EXONERATION FINALLY!

The true story of a Vietnam
reporter's fight to prevent
conviction by the US government

TONY PLATTNER

outskirts
press

Table of Contents

Prologue

This is a fascinating chronicle of perseverance, ingenuity and true grit shown by an acclaimed journalist who revealed early in the Vietnam War the inept handling of the conflict by President Lyndon B. Johnson and then was persecuted for it by his Defense Department. The ongoing efforts to convict him as a criminal under the Espionage Act and then administratively discharge him from the Marine Reserves took place over many years before he was finally exonerated.

I was the reporter and was employed by *Aviation Week & Space Technology* magazine. They had sent me to Vietnam in the fall of 1965 as a combat correspondent to report on the progress of the air war in that conflict.

The titanic struggle that ensued pitted me as a civilian reporter who served as a Marine reservist against the Justice Department, Defense Department and two major services the Navy and the Marine Corps.

The government's case against me hinged on a series of fourteen articles written by me for *Aviation Week*. The series was highly regarded for its detailed observations and predictions on the stalled progress early in the war and the forecast of a lengthy period of conflict yet to come without significant changes in strategy. It turned out that most of the predictions actually turned out to be accurate by the time the conflict ended in 1975.

The concocted charge brought against me was that I had published classified information without authorization with the implication that

I had used my status as a Marine Reserve pilot to illegally obtain classified secrets.

Fighting back against the injustice of the government's effort to convict me as a criminal for doing nothing more than being a capable reporter who played meticulously by the rules required a great deal of help from others, ranging from many congressmen to a well-known lawyer, F. Lee Bailey.

I had flown as a weekend warrior with the Marine Reserve since the fall of 1956 after serving four years of active duty. I continued my reserve flying until February 1967 when, during a phone call from Headquarters of the Marine Corps, I was summarily taken off flying status by the Marine Corps Commandant with no explanation offered. This was about a year after the publication of my series, which ran in late 1965 and early 1966, some nine months after Johnson authorized formal entry of the United States into the war.

After being removed from flying status, I enlisted the help of my California congressional representatives to begin untangling the mystery behind this devastating directive. Partial details of the government's case against me first came to light in a letter from the commandant of the Marine Corps to my congressman, Charles Wiggins, dated Aug. 25, 1967, which said, in part: *"Initial action on this matter was taken on 25 February 1966 when the Director for Security Review, Office of the Assistant Secretary of Defense (Public Affairs), referred the case to the Directorate for Inspection Services (DINS). This referral was in accordance with the responsibilities of the Directorate for Inspection Services concerning unauthorized disclosures of classified defense information.*

"Subsequently, the matter was investigated by the Directorate for Inspection Services, the Naval Investigative Service and the Office of Special Investigations, U.S. Air Force. Results of these investigations were forwarded to the Federal Bureau of Investigation for an opinion concerning prosecution. Additional information developed

by the Directorate for Inspection Services was forwarded to the assistant attorney general by the Federal Bureau of Investigation on 5 May 1967."

Being under the scrutiny of so many investigative agencies in DOD, plus the DOJ, came as a devastating surprise. It also was a powerful indication of the deadly seriousness of those pursuing the case against me. Nevertheless, at the time, I could not conceive how they could have arrived at this conclusion since I was sure that I had never violated any military security regulations, nor had I violated any of the criteria governing how journalists could report on the war in Vietnam.

I strongly believed that I had been classified as a criminal with no evidence to back it up, but taking on the Defense establishment to prove my innocence turned out to be a far more difficult path than I could imagine at the time. Nevertheless, I vowed to myself that I would fight the shadowy opponents hiding behind a veil of military secrecy with a goal of complete exoneration using whatever resources that I could lay my hands on.

Looking back on my conflict with the Defense Department after many years, I realized that there was a fascinating David and Goliath story to be told, and I began research on this book after reviewing the collection of copious notes and documents that had been stored in a footlocker in my attic for over fifty years.

To gain some perspective on how various US Commanders in chief performed during the lengthy thirty-year Vietnam War from the end of World War II to the close of the conflict in 1975, I added a short history of how the US was drawn into this unpopular cold war proxy fight in the far-away jungles of Southeast Asia. I had hoped that this would provide some insight into the enormous pressures against me, but it was not until I began writing the book that the nature of the opposition gradually emerged from the fog of secrecy.

Preparing to put the book together

The first two years were spent researching to gain greater familiarity with the tortured Southeast Asia conflict and to understand our Vietnam involvement from the commander in chief's viewpoint since, at that time, I believed that those behind the effort to convict me were at or near that level. But this is not a historical piece on the Vietnam War since many have done that job in well researched and annotated books, many of which I read as background.

I did attend a symposium in Washington, D.C., on the air war in Vietnam and spent time at the National Archives there as well. The symposium provided a great deal of detail on the many facets of the air war, but my tour of the archives, perhaps due to my limited experience working this source, produced very little. Then I prodded elements in the Defense and Justice Departments through The Freedom of Information Act but was disappointed with the complete lack of forthcoming information. Perhaps more attention to this avenue of pursuit using legal assistance may have produced more information, but I chose not to go this route for financial reasons.

Computer research online, however, proved useful, and I read the now-declassified Pentagon Papers from start to finish as well as other meaningful documents. But the foundation for this story about my battle to clear my name grew directly from a lengthy review of my papers and a careful stitching together of the events and the time lines from my notes and documents.

To set the stage for the telling of my battle with the Defense Department, I added a short preface tracing the long Cold War involvement of the US from the 1940s to the 1970s with an emphasis on the role of aviation since this was the focus of my Vietnam reporting. One of the best sources for this turned out to be the Pentagon Papers which were based on classified documentation located in Defense Department files at the time. The Papers were declassified by the Defense Department in 2011.

The Pentagon Papers were augmented by various histories, among others, Henry Kissinger's 635-page book, *Ending the Vietnam War,* which included discussions of how both Johnson and Nixon handled the war.

Most of the Vietnam War histories focus on how the warfighters on the ground fought against the enemy in his jungle environment, drawing on aviation assets as necessary to win the day, which invariably happened. The ground forces, of course, deserve every recognition for facing the tenacious Viet Cong and North Vietnamese day in and day out on the battlefield and should be credited accordingly for their heroic efforts.

My involvement was to chronicle how the aviation warriors functioned in the conflict and revealed how poorly the Johnson administration handled the air war.

The short recap of the United States' Vietnam involvement adds some perspective to the rationale behind why the various commanders in chief from President Truman on felt compelled to try to blunt the communist expansion in Southeast Asia during the lengthy Cold War. It also highlights some of the early key events that had been all but forgotten by the time the war came home to the American people via the daily papers and evening news in the mid- to late 1960s.

1

A short history of events leading up to and ending the Vietnam War

In 1945, following World War II, when the Japanese were in charge of Indochina, the victorious US agreed to reinstate French sovereignty, putting them in charge again of their former colony. They had ruled it directly for many decades and as a Japanese proxy in World War II. By this time, the communist leader, Ho Chi Minh, who had fought against the Japanese occupiers, was a leader in charge of much of the northern part of the country known as the Democratic Republic of Vietnam (DRV). He also had directed infiltration of a large swathe of the South. He continued to be influential in directing the communist North Vietnamese until he died in 1969.

The French and Ho Chi Minh signed an accord in which the French were allowed reentry to North Vietnam in return for recognition of the DRV as a "free state" as part of the French Union. In April 1946, Indochina's allied occupation (consisting of Vietnam, Laos and Cambodia) was officially terminated. In late 1946, the Franco-Viet Minh war began in earnest. For the next thirty years, the fighting involved massive casualties. The non-communist South Vietnamese with US support clashed with the communist North Vietnamese supported by Communist China and the Communist Soviet Union.

Important related events in Southeast Asia occurred when the Chinese communists under Mao Zedong ousted the Nationalist regime of Chiang Kai-shek from mainland China in 1949. This was soon followed by the start of the Korean War on June 25, 1950.

The Soviet Union was allowed by the US to control the upper half of the Korean Peninsula, separated by the 38th parallel, after its late entry into this region of World War II. The Soviets soon supplied the North Koreans with war equipment and, along with the Chinese, acted as a catalyst for the North Korean invasion of the US-occupied Republic of Korea.

In an innovative move, General MacArthur had the Marine Corps, which was under his command, make an amphibious landing west of Seoul, South Korea's capitol. The landing was made at Inchon as the North Koreans threatened to push the US and its allies out of the Southeast area known as the Busan Perimeter.

This resulted in a turn in the tide of battle, and the Allied forces set their sights on marching to the Yalu River, separating China from North Korea. In a surprise move, however, in October 1950, a massive Chinese army directed by Chairman Mao invaded North Korea, traveling by night and hunkering down by day to avoid detection and then joined the fight alongside the North Koreans against the US and its allies. The result was a stalemate, with neither side being able to dominate the other. The fighting continued for several more years.

Following Stalin's death in the spring of 1953, the USSR backed off from supporting the Korean expansion. As a result, the Chinese support also weakened, and ensuing negotiations led to an Armistice Agreement, which brought the fighting to a halt. On July 27, 1953, the truce was signed with no declared winners or losers, each side retiring to their territory separated by the Demilitarized Zone (DMZ) roughly along the 38th parallel.

By 1954, the military situation in Indochina had deteriorated badly, and the United States believed that another Southeast Asia peninsular-shaped country was in danger of being swallowed up by the communists in the Cold War. After much dialogue, four major players agreed to meet in Geneva, Switzerland, on Feb. 18, 1954, to seek a peaceful solution to Indochina's eight years of war.

The talks were expanded to include nine countries. These were the United States, Great Britain, France, South Vietnam, Laos, Cambodia, the Chinese Peoples Republic, the USSR and the Viet Minh led by Ho Chi Minh.

After months of preliminary talks, the Geneva Accords session with all nine delegates participating for the first time began May 8, 1954, and lasted till July 21. A significant battle that started March 13 at the French Fort of Dien Bien Phu west of Hanoi and near the Laotian border ended in a humiliating defeat for the French on May 7, 1954. The fort had been located to control the flow of men and supplies through Laos to South Vietnam. But the wily North Vietnamese general, Vo Nguyen Giap, with substantial Chinese support, laid siege to the Fort with cleverly placed artillery pummeling the facility and impeding the French ability to resupply the garrison by air.

The French asked the US to intervene, but Commander in Chief, President Eisenhower, who tried to put together a coalition of allies to come to their rescue, failed to field a team and decided against playing a solo role in their defense. The North Vietnamese, with Chinese backing, then scored a humiliating victory over the French defenders.

The final Geneva Accords titled, "Agreement On The Cessation Of Hostilities In Viet-Nam," included the following:

- A two-zone Vietnam separated by a demilitarized zone (DMZ) along the 17th parallel.

- The Vietnamese of the two zones would consult together in July 1955 and reunify Vietnam by national plebiscite one year later (which never took place).
- An International Control Commission (ICC) consisting of representatives from India, Poland and Canada was established to oversee the election and implement the agreement.
- None of the Indochinese States was permitted to join a military alliance or to allow the establishment of foreign military bases on their soil. This meant that the US officially could not introduce military personnel or new equipment or establish bases in any of these countries.

France had already agreed to full independence for the South Vietnamese under Ngo Dinh Diem on June 4, 1954, before the accords were signed. Diem had emerged as the leader of South Vietnam and turned out to be, in some respects, a capable leader with a strong nationalistic focus. He brought a surprising capability to govern to the newly independent South Vietnam country, which, at that time, was plagued by the undercurrents of many opposing forces.

The wave of anticolonialism that surfaced after World War II added to the troubles facing France, as did the loss at Dien Bien Phu, and eventually, the French quit Indochina for good in 1956. This left a vacuum regarding the Geneva Accords, which had awarded France the responsibility for making the truce work and left a weak South Vietnam in charge.

At the time, American thinking and policy-making were dominated by the tendency to view communism in monolithic terms. Therefore, the Viet Minh was seen as part of the Southeast Asia manifestation of the worldwide communist expansion movement. In turn, French resistance to Ho Chi Minh was thought to be a crucial link in the containment of communism.

The espousal of the domino effect supported this strategic

perception of the communist threat: the loss of a single nation in Southeast Asia to communism would inevitably lead to other nations of the area falling under communist control. The Eisenhower administration had first promoted the domino effect at the root of US policy in 1954.

The domino effect had some merit in Indochina. The Viet Minh had already established insurgent forces in Laos and Cambodia, which were fighting the royal governments of both countries. The Chinese were the most important supplier of the Viet Minh, which allowed the Ho Chi Minh communist forces in Vietnam, Laos and Cambodia to thrive. At that time, the communist forces in Laos were known as the Pathet Lao, and those in Cambodia were the Free Khmer (later Khmer Rouge). There were other "dominos" in the region, such as Malaysia, Indonesia, Burma and the Philippines, and these survived their own communist movements with varying degrees of success.

US military advisors and trainers had been present in Vietnam since 1950 under a pentilateral agreement with Laos, Cambodia, Vietnam and France. The US had maintained a Military Advisory Assistance Group (MAAG) in Vietnam since 1950. By 1961, the MAAG in Saigon had grown to 685 personnel, and this was bumped by an additional 175, allowing it to train more Army of the Republic of Vietnam (ARVN) troops. American aid was administered to the South Vietnamese through the MAAG.

In 1956, the South Vietnamese press started to distinguish between the Viet Minh (who desired to be called resistance fighters) and the communists by referring to them as Viet Cong or Vietnamese communists. The new title for the insurgents caught on immediately. The Viet Cong at the time were focusing on gaining control of rural villages and smaller hamlets but gradually moved on to direct action against the Diem military forces and later US forces.

From May 9–15, 1961, Vice President Lyndon Johnson, in a second trip to Vietnam for President Kennedy, said the "battle against communism must be joined in Southeast Asia or throw in the towel." In further recommendations, he suggested that "we proceed with a clear-cut and strong program of action."

There generally followed a lull in the action in 1961. The 1962–'63 period focused on the strategic hamlet program run solely by the Diem government, but not without substantive advice on how to do it from the US. This pacification program aimed to take back the villages and smaller hamlets from the inroads made by the Viet Cong. Diem continued to reject the introduction of active US forces into his country.

The Diem regime, which had successfully resisted any US suggestions for meaningful modifications to its policies, came under heavy fire for its handling of the Buddhist protest demonstrations in Hue on May 8, 1963. Diem's brother Ngo Dinh Nhu played an oppressive role in attacking the Buddhists, including invading their pagodas and jailing many monks. The handling of the Buddhist affair had a significant negative impact on the Diem government's popularity and helped lay the groundwork for the coup that terminated the regime.

Diem became more hardened in his opposition to US advice on reforms that would make his government more efficient, such as an improved intelligence-gathering system. The optimistic field reports based on faulty intelligence in the 1962 and 1963 period of pacification led to a series of erroneous conclusions and a plan for a phased withdrawal by 1965 of US forces.

This policy was formerly quantified in a carefully worded White House announcement on Oct. 2, 1963, that suggested reducing US forces over the next several years while focusing on training the South Vietnamese forces to take over the war effort against the Viet Cong. A month later, on Nov. 1, 1963, Diem and his brother Nhu who had put down the Buddhist uprising, were killed in a coup by South Vietnamese military generals. In the same month, on Nov. 20, 1963, President Kennedy was assassinated.

Within a month, the Diem coup coupled with the resulting political instability and a more realistic assessment of the actual military situation, which showed the Viet Cong much stronger than previously believed, prompted a reevaluation of this questionable strategy and the phased withdrawal idea eventually disappeared.

The US, at a minimum, had a hand in the coup effort in the sense that they tacitly monitored the plotting process by the Vietnamese generals who carried it out from the beginning. This ended a nine-year Diem regime and left in its place a vacuum of uncertainty and an untested group of military people with little experience in running a country.

There were numerous changes of government from 1964 to 1965 that followed as one general after another tried his hand at running the country. Eventually, Air Force Brig. Gen. Nguyen Cao Ky survived in mid-1965.

According to Pentagon Papers authors, "South Vietnam was essentially the creation of the United States. Without US support, Diem almost certainly could not have consolidated his hold on the South during 1955 and 1956. Without US aid in the years following, the Diem regime certainly, and an independent South Vietnam almost as certainly, could not have survived." Consequently, the US had gradually developed a special commitment in South Vietnam and found itself stuck in place with the glue of its own making.

The Pentagon Papers, which were declassified in 2011, provided an exceptional view from inside the Defense Department's Vietnam policies from the end of World War II in 1945 until 1967. They were a report of the OSD (Office of the Secretary of Defense) Vietnam Task Force headed by Leslie H. Gelb and had been commissioned by President Johnson's Defense Secretary. Robert McNamara, on June 17, 1967. The final report was completed on January 15, 1969.

The project began with McNamara's guidance to do studies that were "encyclopedic and objective," with six full-time professionals assigned to complete the work in three months. A year and a half later, and with the involvement of thirty-six professionals, forty-three volumes had been completed. The report was christened with a "TOP SECRET-SENSITIVE" label.

The task force had full access to Defense Department documents as well as CIA materials and some use of State Department cables and memoranda. There was no access to White House files, and personal interviews were not permitted, although reference to news media articles was allowed for perspective. Gelb was proud of the crew that prepared the report and called them "superb—uniformly bright and interested" in his cover letter for the report. He added that they came from everywhere—the military services, State, OSD and the "think tanks." Some stayed for shorter periods due to other commitments.

On June 13, 1971, the *New York Times* published the first open story of the highly classified Pentagon Papers after activist Daniel Ellsberg, who had copied the report, provided them with a portion of the study. Other newspapers, including the *Washington Post,* later joined in, and extensive legal maneuvering got underway as the government tried to prevent further publication.

The Nixon administration charged Ellsberg under Title 17 of the Espionage Act (which later was to be the basis for trying to get me to trial). However, the administration's clumsy handling of the Ellsberg matter, including a break-in by the "plumbers" group to the office of Ellsberg's psychiatrist, helped form the basis for dropping the charges against him.

President Kennedy, followed by President Johnson, were the third and fourth commanders in chief, following Eisenhower and Truman in this leadership role to strongly support halting the communist expansion in Vietnam during the Cold War. A fifth commander in chief, President Nixon, was in charge when negotiations in Paris led to an agreement to end hostilities and release the prisoners of war.

In the early 1960s, the US policy in the conflict was to provide advice and support to its weak South Vietnamese ally, and on August 4 and 5, 1964, the Gulf of Tonkin incident took place. The conflict in international waters between North Vietnamese torpedo boats and US destroyers provided an opportunity for the Johnson administration to inaugurate its use of air power to discourage the North Vietnamese from supporting the Viet Cong effort in the South.

In general, 1964 marked an important reassessment of how to proceed with the Vietnam War. Decisions were made that set the stage for future US policy in the conflict. First, the US awoke to the fact that the Viet Cong were winning the war in the South. Up to this point, the US held firm to the position that its role was to support its South Vietnamese ally who was responsible for defeating the Viet Cong and winning the war.

The Tonkin Gulf incident precipitated the first US reprisal action against North Vietnam with air strikes against naval torpedo boat forces and shipyards that had challenged US Navy destroyers in a "tit-for-tat" retaliatory bombing. This also enabled the Johnson administration to obtain a broad congressional resolution of support.

Throughout 1964, the primary US policy was to severely restrain direct US combat involvement and carry out a psychological campaign to convince Hanoi that it meant business and reassure the South of its steadfast commitment.

There also was confusion over Johnson's reelection campaign rhetoric in which he said he did not intend to lead the United States into a broader war in Vietnam. The election basically called a halt to any aggressive moves by the US in 1964.

Up to early 1965, the US's official position was that the war was a Vietnamese affair. After extensive debate on the issue, Washington announced an air campaign dubbed Rolling Thunder on Feb. 28, 1965. This was to be a continuous, limited air operation against the North to bring about a favorable, negotiated settlement. The first strike was conducted on March 2.

Starting with Rolling Thunder, the bombing campaign was tightly controlled by Washington, and this tight control was to remain in place throughout the Johnson administration. Strikes were carried out only by fighter bombers in low-altitude precise bombing modes. The overall effect of Rolling Thunder was disappointing. US negotiation overtures in Paris had been scornfully rejected. Infiltration had continued and intensified. As a venture in strategic persuasion, the bombing was a dismal failure.

McNamara suggested the expansion of Rolling Thunder in 1965 following a pattern of step-by-step progression. But he rejected the Joint Chiefs of Staff (JCS) concept for fighting the Vietnamese communists by a blockade and mining of the ports. He also vetoed JCS proposals for dramatic attacks on major POL (petroleum, oil and lubricants) depots, power plants, airfields and other "lucrative" targets.

During the bombing pause in which the ten-month Rolling Thunder campaign against North Vietnam was suspended (Dec. 24, 1965, to Jan. 31, 1966) by Johnson, there was a flood of opinions on what steps should be taken to bring about a positive end to the US commitment. These ranged from immediate US withdrawal to putting substantial hurt on the North Vietnamese.

During this phase of the war, Johnson relied heavily on McNamara's input. He dispatched him repeatedly to Saigon to nail down the proper strategy for proceeding with the war. Many voices were heard during the bombing pause, including Dean Rusk's State Department, Military Assistant Command Vietnam's (MACV's) military and State Department leaders, the Joint Chiefs of Staff, Commander in Chief Pacific (CINCPAC) and others. Questions to be resolved included whether to resume bombing and at what level and how much to increase the forces in the South.

Then, in a pivotal turning point, on March 8, 1965, two Marine Battalion Landing Teams arrived in the northern coastal city of Danang to provide security as an initial step toward US commitment. The next month, Johnson threw off the Geneva Accords' self-imposed shackles, which prevented outsiders from introducing new bases, troops, and equipment into the conflict. He approved the proposal to allow US troops in Vietnam in a combat role. He announced it on April 6 and thereby clearly took ownership of the war . . .

The fighting was soon characterized as a US war, although allied forces in the region also joined in, including Australia, South Korea, New Zealand and Thailand.

At this time, the purpose of air strikes against the North was categorized by Secretary Rusk as interdiction and punishment for significant Viet Cong strikes in the South rather than breaking Hanoi's will. This was symptomatic of the ongoing weak nature of the top-down strategy, which was to change many times.

Commander in Chief Johnson approached the war somewhat as a political contest, like working with Congress, trying one thrust after another to influence the unbending Hanoi communists and get them to the bargaining table, none of which had any real effect.

By now, the war's focus had become to win in the South militarily and degrade the flow of men and supplies from North to South.

During this time, the CINCPAC staff put together another strong position on aggressive, renewed bombing of the North, which would close the ports by mining and opening up new targets such as airfields, POL, power plants and others with minimum restrictions. This was soon endorsed by the Joint Chiefs and forwarded on. Others voiced lengthy opinions, laying out some of the possible consequences of aggressive action, such as direct Chinese intervention with troops and the unknown negative reaction of the Soviets.

In part, Johnson's timid approach to the conflict was a fear of "not wanting to start World War III" against the two communist giants, China and the USSR. Concern over the possibility of Chinese troop intervention continued to influence top US decision-makers for many years as they tried to find a workable solution for the troublesome affair.

An example of the overly cautious concern with the possibility of Chinese intervention was the belief which kept airfields with MiG fighters stationed there off the target list based on the fear that bombing them would result in the relocation of the Soviet MiG fighters to Chinese air bases where they could enjoy sanctuary status as they came out to attack US aircraft.

According to the Pentagon Papers, even the strategy of fighting the Viet Cong in the South was questionable at best early in the war. In July 1965, Military Advisory Command Vietnam's (MACV's) optimistic objective to end the war in the Republic of Vietnam (RVN) was to convince the enemy that military victory was impossible and force the enemy to negotiate a solution favorable to the RVN and the US.

With the significant increase of US combat forces in 1965 and 1966, MACV initiated a search and destroy campaign combined with a strong emphasis on body count against the Viet Cong and the growing number of North Vietnamese troops that had filtered into the South, but following the sweep operations, US forces returned to their bases without claiming any new territory. However, MACV stuck to this policy and kept driving in the direction of a pacification program to regain control of the countryside aided by Vietnamese ARVN forces.

Despite fighting a determined and clever insurgent enemy in unfamiliar jungle terrain, US forces almost always prevailed in individual battles. The warfighters on the ground benefitted greatly from support by rotary and fixed-wing aviation, plus highly mobile artillery assets unavailable to the communists in the South and invariably turned the tide of battle.

The reluctance of the White House to approve targets of significance in the North is another story. It is illustrated by first-time strikes on Apr. 20, 1967, of Haiphong power plants, and on Apr. 24, 1967, the bombing of two MiG-based airfields for the first time. On June 11, 1967, the Kep Airfield was attacked for the first time, and ten MIGs were destroyed. This was over two years after the bombing campaign in the North began.

On Mar. 31, 1968, Johnson withdrew as a candidate for president in the upcoming election, leaving the war no closer to a negotiated resolution than when he took command in 1963. Republican Richard Nixon won the election in that fall.

When Commander in Chief Richard Nixon took over, the war moved into more aggressive phases, including dealing with the sanctuaries on South Vietnam's borders directly with the US providing bombing support for mostly South Vietnamese ground troops. Nixon also continued to draw down US forces, and by August 1972, many of the combat forces had left. This was spelled out in Henry Kissinger's book *Ending the Vietnam War,* which described the efforts to bring the North Vietnamese to meaningful peace talks, which had an unproductive history under Johnson.

Frustration at the US High Command level finally reached its peak with the reluctant North Vietnamese. On May 8, 1972, Nixon approved for the first time the mining of the harbors in North Vietnam and a more intensive bombing campaign known as Linebacker I. The mining bottled up twenty-seven ships in the Haiphong Harbor, which remained there until the mines were cleared in July 1973, over a year later. This halted the maritime pipeline for the bulk of supplies that the North Vietnamese depended on to continue the war against the South.

By the fall of 1972, the North Vietnamese were having a hard time supporting their recent offensive launched against the South and suffered from the lack of imported supplies and the heavier aerial bombardment. On October 8, 1972, US National Security Adviser Henry Kissinger and Le Duc Tho, the North Vietnamese negotiator, finally arrived at a general agreement after both sides made concessions.

However, when the negotiations once again stalled in the following months, mainly because South Vietnamese President Nguyen Van

Thieu would not agree to the arrangement, Nixon initiated an even more intensive Linebacker II bombing campaign on December 18, 1972. This included large flights of the huge B-52 bombers striking the areas around Hanoi and Haiphong (albeit with some notable US aircraft losses—although near the end, the risk was reduced after the North had used up their supply of SAMs, which came in by ship).

This broke the logjam. On January 27, 1973, the newly reelected Nixon announced a negotiated agreement between the sides, which brought home the US prisoners, mainly flight crews, in the next few months and basically put an end to US involvement. All of this took place without China's entry into the conflict against US combat forces as once had been feared.

A war-weary US continued to be besieged by protesters, who were noisy and heavily supported by the media. Decision-makers at the very top did not always listen to them, however. One of the negatives of the antiwar movement was the abuse of returning warfighters, unlike the friendly welcome home greetings notable in World War II.

Congress enacted legislation to curtail any further active military involvement in the conflict. The North Vietnamese then descended on the South with fresh supplies. Congress substantially cut its support for the South Vietnamese government in the wake of Nixon's resignation because of Watergate.

Following the clearance of the mines in July 1973 by Navy and Marine Corps helicopter sweepers, the ports once again became a hub of activity, and the highly motivated and patient North Vietnamese mounted a massive military campaign with tanks, artillery and other weapons against the South.

The civil war between the communist Vietnamese and the noncommunist Vietnamese continued for almost two more years. Finally, the last Marine Corps helicopter evacuation flight from the US Embassy in Saigon took place on April 30, 1975, putting final closure on US involvement there.

On that same day, the North Vietnamese flag was raised in Saigon, completing the communist takeover of Vietnam. The two other countries that comprised Indochina, Laos and Cambodia, soon fell to communist forces as the domino effect predicted.

The toll among our nation's young warriors was crushing. As of May 2018, there were 58,320 names engraved on the black granite walls of the Vietnam Veterans Memorial in Washington, D.C. Only the names were listed in chronological order without any other inscriptions. This provided in one location a record of the combat and noncombat deaths and the missing in action of the men and women who went to war and did not return.

But beyond the names on that wall, many of those who returned home would live with various scars of battle that would plague them for lengthy periods. Besides the typical combat injuries such as embedded shrapnel and loss of limbs, there was post-traumatic stress disorder (PTSD) and the cancerous aftereffects of Agent Orange used to defoliate the jungles where the enemy lurked. The Agent Orange effects are still being played out.

One National Vietnam Veterans study estimated that there were 479,612 cases of PTSD among the 3.14 million men and 7,200 women who served, with a high percentage of these mental traumas continuing for years.

The last helicopter flight in Vietnam ended this one of two major proxy conflicts of the Cold War era, which the US fought in Southeast Asia. Many labeled the results of this effort to contain communist Chinese and USSR aggression in simplistic terms as one tie for the Korean truce and one loss in Vietnam. However, this label discredits the valor and determination of the US warriors (and their allies). They went to fight under orders of their government against cold war foes and performed notably and at great sacrifice for their country. It also discounts the fact that the communist aggression in this region was blunted for many years after sustaining substantial losses in the lengthy Cold War that took place from shortly after World War II until the collapse of the Soviet Union in 1991.

The North Vietnamese in 1995, whose tenacity was continuously underestimated by the US until the end, announced that their military had suffered over one million killed.

2

Joining the Marine Corps and going to work for *Aviation Week*

My early years in the depth of the Depression-racked 1930s began at the Walker, Minnesota, hospital where I was born May 29, 1930. My father had been the chief salesman for the giant Mascot A Ranch silver fox farm on the north shore of Webb Lake near Hackensack, Minnesota. The "Ranch," as it was called, was built up during the roaring '20s when wearing silver fox furs was popular.

My grandfather, Arthur F. Maeser, an innovative entrepreneur, founded it. He and his wife, Amy Maeser, had two daughters, Hope and Ethelwynne, and a son, Arthur. My father married Ethelwynne in 1928 when the Ranch was near the crest of its financial performance. But the stock market crash of 1929, the Depression and other factors took a heavy toll on the Ranch. It spiraled downward into a receivership mandate, allowing the owners to live on the property while paying off debts to investors.

The personal finances of my father and mother also took a hit. Shortly after I was born, my parents severed their relationship with the Ranch and packed their belongings, along with me, in the back of their car. They headed west to the state of Montana, where they founded a fox ranch of their own. They settled in Colorado Gulch outside of Helena, Montana, in the midst of the Rocky Mountains, and began raising silver foxes along with a partner, Leo Zimmer.

After several years in the log cabin where we lived with no electricity, a wood cookstove, Coleman lanterns and water only available by bucket from a local stream, the problem of schooling my younger brother, John, and I became apparent, given our sometimes snow-bound situation in the heart of the school year. After much discussion and negotiation, a decision was made to return to my grandfather's fox ranch on Webb Lake, Minnesota.

The Ranch was still raising foxes, although at a much-slower pace in receivership mode, which later required that many of the structures of the onetime showpiece community be torn down and sold off.

My parents' job at the Ranch was operating the Northern Minnesota Publishing Company, which my grandfather had established as part of his growing empire to control the local press. The main business was three weekly newspapers and handling the printing needs of the community.

The Ranch's concept of operations pioneered by my grandfather in the early 1920s was to sell investors a mating pair of silver foxes for $1,000, which were then raised at the Ranch. When they had ongoing litters, they were sold back to the Ranch, and the investors reaped the profits.

The Ranch was a self-contained, small village that had become what was claimed to be the largest silver fox farm in the world during the prosperous 1920s. Among its assets were five units each, with hundreds of fox pens. They were supported by the latest technology in feeding and medical facilities. Several on-site veterinarians ensured that the latest medical knowledge was available.

A large powerhouse was accompanied by a towering brick

chimney and a central steam heating plant and two diesel electrical power generators. Some of the key buildings were connected by underground tunnels, protecting against the frigid Minnesota winters.

Also included were a gas station with a small store and soda fountain, a boathouse with a high-speed runabout, and on the second floor of the publishing company building was a dance hall and a fully-equipped stage to view plays and movies. A series of resort cottages around the shore of the lake brought in tourist income.

Such extravagances as a personal airplane and pilot, a Lincoln Town Car with chauffeur and a 105-foot yacht berthed in Seattle used for keeping tabs on a remote fox ranch on an island in Alaska were an early target of the receivership supervisors.

Within a few years of my arrival at the Ranch, I was thrust into the labor force run by my grandfather. He was a stern, old-school German taskmaster who booked no foolishness in his workers. He paid my brother John and me ten cents a day until John went on strike for a negotiated raise to fifteen cents per day.

I was assigned chores every day of the year and full-time summer work in the farm fields that supported the Ranch. This early exposure to the daily chores of farm work baked into my psyche a strong work ethic that never left me.

By the time I was thirteen years old, my parents had encountered substantial problems meeting the weekly newspapers' deadlines due to the erratic reliability of the Ranch's failing electrical power-generating system. With no alternative, my parents moved the publishing company to the nearby village of Walker in 1943.

At the Walker School, I was an eager participant in all school activities—sports (football and basketball), student council president, choir, band and editor of the senior yearbook. Unfortunately, I was only a fair student, and I came to regret this careless attention to learning soon after entering Carleton College in Northfield, Minnesota, in 1948. Carleton was a small, highly ranked liberal arts school populated with many valedictorians and salutatorians from big-city schools, making classroom curves a monumental challenge for me.

I was immediately placed in the "bonehead" English class and struggled to survive my first semester. Near the end, and faced with dropping below a C average, I completed a "Hail Mary" miraculous save in chemistry by acing the final test with an A, which kept me in school with the required minimum average. I slowly but consistently improved my academic record and graduated with a math major and physics minor, with an acceptable grade level.

In my junior year, the Korean War, along with its draft require-ments, began in June 1950, but I remained in school with an educa-tion exemption until graduation in June 1952. Then I immediately received a message to report to my local draft board. With four years of hard studying behind me and a Bachelor of Arts degree in hand, there was no enthusiasm for serving as a draftee, so I began looking at other options.

There was a tradition of military service in my family. My brother, John, a year and a half younger, had quit school at Bemidji State Teachers College and volunteered during the Minnesota National Guard call-up in 1951 for the Korean War. He became an airborne ranger and served a combat tour in Korea.

My father had served in the navy in World War I and was an active veteran in the American Legion and as a service officer for the county. An uncle was a career army officer who entered the service before World War II and later was buried in Arlington National Cemetery, so the military tradition in our family was well established.

With a fine college education behind me and being relatively fit—I was a quarterback in football and a basketball guard in high school, and in college, I had been captain of the ski team—I turned to what appeared to be the most challenging option, naval aviation. Navy flyers were faced with operating to and from floating airfields and seemed to be the cream of the military's aviators.

Within days of my graduation in early June 1952, I went down to the Naval Air Station in Minneapolis and signed up for the Naval Aviation Cadet (NAVCAD) program.

The physical exam, particularly the eye test, was a tough one—it weeded out many candidates. According to the officials who administered the tests, I passed both the physical and mental exams with good grades. Soon, I was notified that I should report to NAS Pensacola on August 30, 1952, to begin the preflight phase.

Preflight training was sixteen weeks of classroom, physical training and learning the basics of military drilling and discipline. Flying would come later. We had to pass a class A swimming test and survive the Dilbert Dunker, a simulated cockpit that rode down a rail into the pool with you buckled in, and then, inverted under the water, you were required to unbuckle and determine which way to swim to the surface. There also were boxing, wrestling and other physical challenges, complemented by military discipline and schooling.

In the classroom, we learned navigation, including celestial and dead reckoning—this was long before modern navigation aids. I enjoyed this course and had one of the highest scores in our class of fifty-four students. Weather, power plants (mainly piston engines), aeronautical engineering, and naval orientation, which recalled the glory of past naval activities, were part of the syllabus.

As a naval aviation cadet, I held a rank in the no-man's land midway between an enlisted petty officer and a warrant officer and drew a salary of $98 a month. In preliminary training, we weren't allowed to use the Officers' Club, relegated, instead, to a beer bar called the AKRack. When we progressed to advanced training, we were allowed into the O Club.

The next of many moves was to nearby Whiting Field, where the North American SNJ trainer and basic flying maneuvers, including the critical solo flight, awaited. The SNJ was a rugged, tandem-seat trainer equipped with a tail wheel to refine your three-point landing technique for carrier landings. Continued progress included instrument flying, formation, gunnery and carrier landing basics.

My first and only accident occurred while preparing to go aboard the carrier in the last phase of basic before going on to advanced training. At Baron Field, I was doing Field Carrier Landing Practice (FCLP) flights when the normally reliable Pratt & Whitney engine quit. I was several hundred feet above the ground in a high-drag state with gear and flaps down as I approached the simulated carrier landing site.

I became an instant missile, and after a quick check of all the controls, such as the mixture, to see if I had forgotten anything, I tried my best to steer the downward plummeting SNJ to a landing. I was only partially successful, however, and the bird hit a wingtip first, then cartwheeled, striking the engine which came off, and what was left of the airplane, fortunately, came to rest upright.

When the engine separated, a fire started at the firewall, and since the canopy already was open, I hastily began my exit. Earlier, when I entered the FCLP pattern, I had forgotten to unlatch the leg straps of the parachute which we sat on, so my departure from the airplane and then from the vicinity to avoid a potential explosion was a bit clumsy with the chute dragging behind me, still attached to the leg harnesses—it must have presented a strange sight.

After separating myself from the chute, a helicopter crew picked me up and provided a couple of mini bottles of bourbon during the flight to the base hospital. The crew commented on how calm I appeared right after the mishap. I was examined and given a thumbs-up by the flight surgeon. After a speedy disposition board, I was returned to flying status and rejoined my group, continuing on to perform the requisite number of arrested landings on the carrier. This completed the basic phase.

At the end of basic, I needed to decide: become a Marine Corps flyer or a Navy flyer—both were naval aviators. I had already made up my mind to join the Marine Corps after listening to a stirring speech by a marine captain who spoke about the prospect of single-engine attack and fighter flying in the Corps. At the time, it was rumored that most navy-choice NAVCAD candidates were heading to fly amphibians on boring patrol and antisubmarine warfare missions, which helped clinch my decision.

After leaving Pensacola, I checked in for advanced training at NAS Corpus Christi in Texas. I was assigned to the VA attack syllabus at Cabaniss Field, flying the Grumman F6F Hellcat—the renowned navy fighter of World War II—and a wonderful bird she was. Lady Fortune also smiled on me by assigning me to a very talented group of fledgling aviators and a great navy LTJG instructor. This was one of the most memorable flying periods that I enjoyed in my career as an aviator and involved occasional flying as a six-plane formation in Blue Angel-like maneuvers.

Following Corpus Christi, I returned to Pensacola for carrier qualification in the Hellcat. I went through the field carrier landing flights that used a carrier deck outline painted on the runway to prepare you for coming on board the carrier under the direction of a landing signal officer (LSO). The LSO, located on the port side of the carrier near the stern, was equipped with a radio and paddles used to guide you through the landing phase with various paddle signals such as high, low, slow, fast and wave off.

In the cockpit, the pilot faced the challenge of maintaining the right speed a few knots above stall, then descending at the proper downward rate to reach a runway that was continuously moving away. All of this had to be done by maintaining visual contact with the LSO and responding to his signals. A skillful combination of stick and power settings was needed and accomplished without the angle of attack indication or the yet-to-come lens system, which provided a glide slope and simplified the carrier landing task.

Then the day of the final training event arrived, and our flight flew out to the carrier. On my initial landing, which was a three-point plunge to the deck with power off to catch an early wire, all went well . . . at first. After snubbing to a stop, the plane captain gave me a surprising wing-fold signal, and at the same time, the carrier's operations officer said, "Iron 43 (my call sign), you have just cost the navy $45,000." Then the signals came swiftly, and I was directed to the elevator and swished down to the lower deck. There, I was directed to depart the aircraft and was sent to an empty ready room to await my fate.

At stake here was graduation from the navy flight training program and going home for Christmas as a second lieutenant with naval aviator wings or some unknown future that, at worst, could send me to the fleet as a seaman to finish up my tour. I was unable to find fault with my carrier landing, so I just stewed for an hour or so about the mysterious situation awaiting some input on the meaning of it all.

Finally, the LSO for our flight arrived along with the other Hellcat pilots in my flight, and I listened to their debriefings. Eventually, the LSO turned to me and explained what had happened. The F6F has a lower lip on the engine cowl that acts as an air scoop for the oil cooler. Although part of the preflight is peering into this scoop to see if it was empty of debris, I always had a hard time jumping high enough to get a good look, being only five foot eight.

It turned out that someone left a leather mallet in the scoop, and when the plane decelerated after catching a hook, the mallet surged forward into the propeller and flew high into the air. This caused the carrier operations officer to mistakenly assume that I had put on the brakes, nosed over and hit the wooden deck with the prop causing debris to fly into the air—thus requiring an expensive repair.

After matter-of-factly describing what had happened, the LSO asked me if I wanted to finish qualifying with the flight. I tried to control my relief at this fortunate turn of events and appear nonchalant as I immediately accepted the offer to climb back into the cockpit.

I found that my flying skills had not been diminished by the setback and went on to complete the required number of six arrested landings and two catapult shots and flew back to the beach the same day. The admiral pinned on my golden wings and second lieutenant bars at a graduation ceremony within a short time, and I proudly went home for Christmas.

After the holidays, I returned to Corpus Christi for all-weather flight training in the twin-engine Beechcraft SNB. I mastered the art of flying with only reference to cockpit instruments as well as recovering from the effects of vertigo. At the time, the navy relied on the Adcock navigational aid to work the approaching aircraft through the soup to the airfield. This consisted of a set of crossed beams using the Morse code N (dah dit) and A (dit dah) quadrants on either side of the beams for orientation. Along the beams and where they crossed in the center, silence prevailed, providing clues as to where you were. This complicated method of flying in the clouds was a far cry from the much-improved modern navigation aids, but it provided a tool at the time to conduct flight operations in foul weather.

Then it was off to Marine Corps Air Station Cherry Point, North Carolina, for my first fleet assignment, VMC-2, flying Douglas AD-4N and AD-5W Skyraiders. Upon check-in, I was told by a friend of mine in administration that I had the highest score he had seen coming from flight training.

Since I had flown Hellcats, checkout was easy in the propeller-driven ADs equipped with special radars. I enjoyed flying the AD and the squadron life with many of the pilots who had been called up as reservists in the Korean War and were finishing up their tours. But jet aircraft called me, and I soon signed up to get checked out in the training squadron.

After I finished up the jet syllabus in Grumman F9F Panthers, I was ordered to Korea. Combat flying had officially ended with the signing of the Armistice on July 27, 1953, but a marine air wing was still stationed at K-3 air base on the east coast. I arrived there in November 1954 for a fourteen-month tour and was assigned to VMF-115, an F9F-5 straight-wing Panther jet squadron. Flying in combat is the ultimate goal of every marine aviator—as it was mine—but through the fate of timing, I had missed this opportunity by sixteen months.

Peacetime flying in-country was not without its challenges and required careful attention to detail. I recall one DMZ reconnaissance mission in which I was on instruments in my F9F-5 shortly after take-off until I touched down in a ground-controlled approach (GCA) to virtually zero ceiling and visibility at the K-3 airfield and taxied slowly back to the flight line in the fog. The Panther Jet was not fitted with autopilot and had only a low-frequency homing radio for navigation. This required constant attention during the entire mission to change radio frequencies, navigate from point to point while flying at assigned flight levels in the soup. Training accidents also were a reality, and a friend of mine who had only been in the unit a short time augured into the ground with possible oxygen problems. Another friend from my NAVCAD class who had gone navy after primary crashed into the water off the coast and was never recovered.

After my squadron returned stateside to Marine Corps Air Station (MCAS) El Toro the following May, I finished up my tour at MACS-3, a Marine Corps Air Control Squadron which needed aviators as controllers. I was assigned as the electronics officer and also assistant operations officer. I sharpened up my shooting eye on weekends, hunting pheasants and ducks, and took advantage of every rest and recreation opportunity, including two trips to Hong Kong, where I participated in the customary low-cost clothing purchases, among other pursuits.

After closing my Korean tour, I reported to Marine Corps Air Station (MCAS), El Toro. Since I was a marine reservist with only eight months till the end of my tour on August 30, 1956, I was assigned to a headquarters squadron and given the job of special services officer for Air FMFPAC. I later received a letter of accommodation from the commanding general when I departed for my reserve assignment. I had deliberately elected not to "go regular," which would have required signing up for an additional tour of duty since I wanted to continue my military career in the reserves.

It is perhaps important to note some basics about the Marine Corps. The "Corps" is an organization run by the ground forces that directly take on the enemy in combat. Their long history is legendary and filled with countless stories of courage and heroism, and the warfighters always have earned the country's utmost respect and admiration.

The Corps is a relatively light infantry force during amphibious operations, which is a foundational mission. As such, they rely heavily on their integral air assets not only for rotary-wing mobility but also for fixed-wing close air support on the battlefield. The Corps traditionally task organizes, which emphasizes teamwork of its integral elements, including its air assets. Thus fixed-wing aviation is always an essential part of any Marine Corps operation.

The marine's air force consists of three regular air wings and one reserve air wing (which I was a part of as a weekend warrior) and is paired with three regular and one reserve divisions. All of this is augmented by a sizable logistics organization.

In September 1956, following my four years of active duty, I was transferred to NAS Twin Cities, where I joined a reserve squadron flying first F9F-5s and later AD-5s. That fall was a busy period since I had signed up to get a master's degree in journalism at the University of Minnesota and got married at the same time. While at El Toro, I had met a stunningly beautiful woman of Hispanic heritage and finally convinced her to marry me.

At the end of the quarter in January 1957, plans changed, and I gave up on my further education. Helen and I, along with her two young daughters from a previous marriage, Gail and Francine, jumped in a car and headed west to California, where I got a job as an associate engineer for Marquardt Aircraft Co.

During this year-long period in Van Nuys, we added Anthony, our first son, to the family mix. At the end of 1957, we all returned to Walker, Minnesota, where I joined the family newspaper business with my father and mother, a move that had long been discussed with my parents. And I checked back into the Minneapolis reserve squadron.

Reserve flying was little different from active duty flying and required continued vigilance. One cold winter drill weekend in January, I was tasked with flying an A-1E single-engine attack airplane from the Minneapolis Naval Air Station to Cheyenne, Wyoming, to ferry an aircraft part. While en route over the bleak South Dakota landscape, the engine stopped, and I immediately transitioned into a glider on a one-way trip to the ground.

It had recently snowed, and the prairie landscape was as white as a bed sheet, making it very difficult to pick out safe, potential landing sites, such as a road or a field that was free of gullies and other hazards. I was almost two miles above the earth at a 12,000-foot altitude when the big 2,500 HP Wright engine became silent. The whoosh of the wind over the wings and around the cockpit replaced the comforting drone of the engine. Survival depended on gliding to a safe landing site, but the limited odds of this happening gave me little hope of success.

I quickly went through the emergency procedures of reducing drag by putting the big fourteen-foot prop in high pitch, establishing a ninety-five kt. best glide speed, and putting out a Mayday call on the emergency frequency. I tried numerous times to restart the engine without any success while continuing my frantic search for a safe landing spot where I could save the airplane as well as myself.

Suddenly, with great relief, I heard a friendly voice on the radio's 243.0 megahertz frequency asking if they could help. I requested directions to an airfield where I could make an engine-out landing and was given a vector to the tower I was speaking with. I was lucky to be relatively close to the air base, and, combined with the excellent glide ratio of the Skyraider, I had enough altitude to make a 360-degree overhead approach, put the gear down in the final and touch down for a no-flaps emergency landing near the end of the runway.

On the rollout, I was preparing to stop and wait for a tow when suddenly, the engine started up again. I taxied to the apron, called back to the detachment and discussed the situation. Although I had followed the handbook on the carburetor heat requirements, it had iced up outside of the identified range, perhaps due to a meteorological abnormality. Then the ice had melted during my descent, allowing the wind-milling engine to restart. I flew back to Minneapolis after aborting the Cheyenne mission with a feeling of profound relief, deep gratitude for the assistance of the alert tower operator and full carburetor heat.

By 1962, I had lived in Walker, Minnesota, for four years flying with the Marine Reserves at Minneapolis and working in my parents' weekly newspaper publishing company. At the strong urging of my parents, I had joined them, making it a family affair. However, my work was primarily that of a printer since my parents were immersed in the management and reporting end of the newspaper business, although I did some limited reporting.

By 1962, my family had expanded to five wonderful children: Tony, Michael and Jacqueline, as well as Gail and Francine. However, I began having second thoughts about my commitment to the family enterprise. The future did not look promising financially, and I started thinking about college education for the kids.

I had a hard time paying bills on my near-poverty-level wages. I was primarily a printer running automatic printing presses and immersed in the time-consuming weekly task of producing three local newspapers using the labor-intensive process of hot type (linotype) and a Miehle rotary printing press from the 1920s. The pay for flying in the Marine Reserves was the only thing that kept me afloat.

Added to this conundrum was the fact that my parents' only retirement income would come to them when they sold the business, and I had no realistic means of raising the substantial sum of money needed to buy them out.

I had been a longtime subscriber to the world aviation's leading news magazine, *Aviation Week & Space Technology*. After four years of treading water at the Northern Minnesota Publishing Co., I decided to try a challenging forward leap to become a reporter for them. The fact that I had never held a job as a daily newspaper reporter (which the magazine strongly desired) did not deter me from my new crusade.

I put in a phone call to the magazine's managing editor, Bill Gregory, explaining my willingness to come to work for them. Surprisingly, after some conversation, he asked me to fly to New York for an interview at their expense. Although I was weak in reporting experience, on the positive side, I had graduated from one of the top-rated liberal arts schools in the country with a degree in math and a minor in physics. I had worked for a period as an engineer and had recent flight experience as a marine aviator.

After meeting with Gregory, a World War II navy pilot, he sent me on to Washington, D.C., to speak with Editor Bob Hotz, who had served in China with the Flying Tiger contingent. I returned to Walker feeling optimistic about the visit and shortly received a phone call from Hotz with a suggestion that I turn in a couple of stories based on some technical papers they would send me—my limited reporting experience was on the table.

It turned out to be a tough test. I labored intently at the typewriter long hours into the evenings for a couple of weeks, falling victim to a bad case of eyestrain. This resulted in a short grounding of my reserve flying until my eyes recovered, and I was returned to flight status. I tried to make sense of several rather obscure technical papers presented at engineering symposiums to turn them into readable stories. I went over them repeatedly, trying to hone my writing skills, and finally achieved some limited success. After typing up a final version, I shipped them off and waited for the call, and it soon came with an offer to go to work for them at a salary more than twice as grand as I was making.

My parents, of course, were devastated. Still, the die was cast, and I spent the next five months in the magazine's New York Bureau learning to report the *Aviation Week* way at the "big green" McGraw-Hill building on W. Forty-Second Street in downtown Manhattan. Since I was living in New York by myself, I devoted seven days a week to the task of clawing upward toward the goal of becoming an investigative journalist who could hold his own at the magazine.

That was a lofty target indeed and kind of like the challenge I faced in the navy flight training program. It was founded on accuracy, readability, digging deep for details and coming up with new information that had yet to see print. It also meant joining and competing with an elite reporting staff.

Bob Hotz, who I worked for, was one of the most respected journalism bosses in the country at the time and a stern taskmaster sometimes with the discipline of a drill instructor. But he was equally quick to compliment you when he approved of your product.

Several months into my New York tour of duty, I began searching for a breakout story that would provide my boss with confidence to allow me to head for a permanent staff location in Los Angeles, where I could relocate my family. The navy's A2F (later A-6A) all-weather attack aircraft seemed like an ideal target since almost nothing had been written about it, and it was nearing the end of its development cycle.

I phoned the manufacturer, Grumman Aircraft, to make

arrangements—the magazine's reporters were mainly responsible for initiating their own stories. Grumman was receptive and pleased that *Aviation Week* was interested, and I visited the factory on Long Island with my ever-present notebook and pen in hand. I interviewed the Grumman team members, who had been cleared to speak with me by the navy, which provided the article's primary sources.

After long hours at the typewriter, I worried the story into its final form. I made some callbacks to check on details and received some help from other staff members who filled in some of the holes in the story. I searched for all the tidbits of information that had been in print (which were very few). Then I used the handout material to illustrate the emphasis on avionics in this revolutionary new aircraft.

A design analysis was needed, so I used the interconnecting diagram of the major subsystems that had been provided and arrived at a pretty good description of how the airplane could perform its air-to-ground mission under visual flight rules (VFR) as well as at night and in poor weather under instrument flight rules (IFR). This gave the navy the capability of attacking targets on an around-the-clock basis in any kind of weather, a brand-new boost for its floating airfields.

To wrap it up, I faced the challenge of describing the performance—speed, endurance, altitude, etc. These details generally had not been available during my Grumman interviews.

Performance numbers always are an issue with new aircraft. The airframe companies would like to keep such data quiet for as long as possible, if for no other reason than keeping the competition in the dark on their design. From the military's standpoint, they want to keep such information from enemy forces to maintain a combat edge.

Lacking hard numbers, I did some educated guessing. I came up with such analytics as endurance approaching a Douglas propeller-driven A-1 and speeds approaching Mach 0.9 (the blunt-nose configuration was not built for supersonic speed). This put the finishing touches on the story, and at that point, I believed I had at least come close to the level of being an investigative *Aviation Week* reporter.

The twin-engine, side-by-side cockpit A-6A Intruder went on to become one of the premium air-to-ground attack aircraft in the US arsenal being flown by both marine and navy pilots on day and night missions under visual and instrument conditions. It was a heavy hauler of weapons with multiple hard points for hanging a wide variety of bombs, rockets, mines and other ordnance. An electronic countermeasures version, the AE-6A, also became an important asset in electronic warfare for detecting and silencing enemy electronics.

Due to its extensive array of electronics, the A2F's large ordnance load and low-level navigation capability were highly valued during the war against North Vietnam. Its capabilities included laying mines, which came to be invaluable in helping close out the US participation in the war by halting the shipping of supplies to the North in 1973.

The article appeared in the Nov. 5, 1962, issue with an upper right-hand cover blurb, "Avionic System Integrated for A2F Mission," calling attention to the story. The article was headlined "Extensive Electronics Aid A2F Capability" by C. M. Plattner. Not long after it appeared, Hotz, who was pleased with it, agreed that I could head for the Los Angeles Bureau.

The A2F story graduated me to the next phase of my *Aviation Week* career—the Los Angeles Bureau, where the listing on the masthead was as an engineering editor. After checking out from the McGraw-Hill Building in late 1962, I collected my family of five children and my dear wife, Helen, and headed west to California again.

Not long after arriving at the McGraw-Hill office in downtown Los Angeles, I received a strange phone call from a voice who identified himself with the Office of Naval Intelligence (ONI). Little did I realize then that this was only the beginning of a long and difficult period in which I would do battle with the Department of Defense and, more specifically, its navy and Marine Corps services for many years over their claim that I had access to and published classified information in my *Aviation Week* articles because of my association with the Marine Reserve.

I immediately took the ONI request to interview me about the Grumman A2F article to the bureau chief, Irv Stone, and he took it to Bob Hotz. After some discussion, they set the ground rules that Irv would have to be in the meeting to represent the magazine, and the ONI representative agreed.

3

The Office of Naval Intelligence Shows up to question me

The Office of Naval Intelligence is a part of the Secretary of the Navy's Department headquartered in the northern Washington, D.C., area in a secure location off Suitland Road in the National Maritime Intelligence Center (NMIC). It is clustered with three other government agencies, including one of the National Archives buildings. The ONI is a secretive organization that gathers maritime intelligence as well as performing other missions.

It contains a group called the Naval Investigative Service (NIS), which consists of a corps of agents with skills in solving criminal matters (sometimes referred to as "gumshoes"). Since their targets come from a vast audience of sailors and marines, their investigations are widespread. They include typical criminal problems such as killings, theft, arson and the like, as well as counterintelligence and catching spies.

The agency's investigative files remain behind closed doors in a perpetually guarded state that provides no opportunity to rebut their findings' accuracy. My efforts to obtain records (estimated at eleven volumes) of files in my case through the Freedom of Information Act in preparation for this book were a flat "no information is available."

At the Los Angeles Bureau meeting on February 7, 1963, when we asked why they were there, the two ONI agents, A. R. Arrigo and R. F. Groth, said that I had published classified information. They wanted to know who my sources were. Agent Arrigo advised me of my rights and said I need not answer questions, but the answers could be used against me if I did. Groth, a navy commander, said the article told about all there was to know concerning the airplane. He would not reveal the specifics that turned the article into a classified document, but the implication was that a good deal was considered classified.

My immediate response to the questions on sources was in line with the code that all good reporters live by—*I can't discuss any specifics on sources for the article*. This was reinforced by Irv Stone, who occasionally intervened when they questioned me, perhaps to the annoyance of the two investigators.

Of course, investigations at Grumman had, by now, undoubtedly, turned up everyone I spoke with while I was there gathering information for the article. Still, under the code, I did not disclose these or any other names to the agents. This resulted in an impasse between the agents and me that shortened the length of the discussion.

By this time, I was concerned over the accusation that I had disclosed classified information. I knew that at no time had anyone I had spoken with given me on or off the record anything identified as secure information. And under the code of the magazine and my own approach to reporting, I always made clear in my interviews that I did not want to have classified information in any way provided to me.

In addition to being a good journalism policy, there was a very practical reason for this. Firstly, there was the basis for handling all secure information which is that a need-to-know requirement must first be established before any access is allowed. And secondly, if classified information were transmitted to me either as a stamped document or verbally described as classified, I would be responsible for ensuring the continued protection of its security and could no longer disclose it in a story in the open press without violating security regulations.

The accusation also ran completely counter to my personal approach to life—playing the game honestly in an aboveboard fashion—it implied that I was using some backdoor method to gather protected information.

Since the agents were naval criminal investigators, the link to my status as a reserve pilot was obviously in play. The navy otherwise would have no jurisdiction over the civilian magazine I worked for. The realization that the navy believed that I had taken advantage of my reserve status to obtain information that fell into a classified category was a direct challenge to my integrity and honesty.

I could not conceive how anyone could develop such a preposterous theory. Up to that point, I had never heard of the NIS. But their presence in the Los Angeles office where I worked could have provided a clue of trouble to come had I been perceptive enough to recognize it—which I wasn't.

Toward the end of our discussions with the agents, and in a somewhat misguided tactic to assuage my offended sense of innocence, I agreed to type out a statement for the agents. This was done against Irv Stone's advice and followed later by Bob Hotz's bombastic response, but I felt so strongly about the accusation that I wanted to make my case in writing. The following excerpt is from my statement:

"To the best of my knowledge, no classified information was received at any time during interviews at Grumman Aircraft Corp., Bethpage, L. I., nor to the best of my knowledge, at the time, did any classified information appear in the article which I wrote on the A2F as described above. Special effort, including double-checking some of the information, was made to preclude publishing any information of

a classified nature, and at no time when I was researching information for the article, which included interviews at Grumman, was classified material given me, which was made known as classified material."

In a memo to Hotz recapping the meeting, I said that there would be no more signed statements in the future. The meeting ended with the disappointed agents leaving with a piece of paper signed by me that denied access to classified information but with no insight on sources. A Marine Corps friend who had experience with the NIS later speculated that the investigators probably labeled me as "noncooperative" in their report. No follow-up contacts with the agents on the Grumman story occurred, although this was not the last time I would see them.

From the navy's standpoint, the A2F up to this point had been conducted behind a wall of secrecy. This is normal in such early development programs for military airplanes. So when my story suddenly appeared and discussed for the first time in print extensive details of the program, it undoubtedly was a shock to those in the navy living by their strict "loose lips sink ships" code.

The murky issue of what constitutes classified information has many facets, one of which is illustrated by the fact that a copy of my article that appeared in an unclassified national publication was, in a stamped version in possession of the agents, a secret document.

This rush to judgment by the navy at the outset of my career with *Aviation Week* was founded solely on suspicion with no evidence to support it. Unfortunately for me, in the years to come, the ability to hide behind the secrecy shroud provided a convenient cover that allowed the navy to continue pursuing their vendetta against me undetected.

In the real world of the reserves, access to classified information was virtually nonexistent since there was no need for it in the process of performing my flying duties.

The following years of reporting in Los Angeles as an engineering editor and the magazine's flight evaluation specialist were character-ized by continuing growth in my writing and reporting skills. I gained generally favorable comments from Hotz in the weekly issue that he marked up with comments on individual stories and circulated to the staff.

I gradually developed news sources in covering many of the events at major aerospace companies such as Boeing, Douglas, Lockheed, Northrop, North American, General Dynamics, Ryan and others, as well as flight testing activities at Edwards Air Force Base. And I contin-ued flying A-4A/B aircraft on weekends at NAS, Los Alamitos.

It's important to characterize the type of reporting I was doing because most of the stories that I wrote discussed the latest tech-nology in the aerospace industry, including military and commercial programs.

My stories described state-of-the-art developments that were ad-vanced well beyond the level represented in the old Douglas A-4A and B aircraft models (the first ones built), which I flew, and subse-quently were provided to Argentina and used by them in the Falklands War.

As a reporter, you learn from every story you write, so you gradu-ally become a skilled interrogator. You can draw from a background of the latest technology in the field you are examining. This allows you to probe deeply in a semiexpert way. Of course, those you in-terview are not always willing to share all the details, but knowing the issues normally leads to as much as can be publicly revealed. Instilling trust with sources was a key to gaining information, and I never violated confidences which, of course, paid off in subsequent dialogues with them.

The one thing that reserve flying did give me was a means of stay-ing current in piloting skills which was useful since I was one of the primary flight evaluation pilots for the magazine.

As a result, at that time, despite the navy's unfounded claim that

I had somehow learned and then published classified information through the benefit of my reserve status, their position seemed so patently ridiculous that neither I nor the magazine's management saw a problem with continuing to be a marine reservist and doing my reporting job.

My skills as a reporter continued to grow, and I was fortunate to be a part of the latest developments in commercial and military aviation on the West Coast. Over the next seven years, I flew or rode along on new aircraft designs of the time, including commercial, military and general aviation airplanes, as well as aircraft simulators. My flying background was mostly in single-engine fighter and attack airplanes with some limited multiengine time, so I was never comfortable applying for a seat in the large three- or four-engine transport aircraft. However, I did fly the medium commercial planes from the left seat, such as the DC-9, 727 and 737.

I also rode along on military aircraft such as the Lockheed F-104 with a Mach 2.0 dash, and I observed the full performance spectrum of the swing-wing General Dynamics F-111. A total of thirty-one of my articles were reprinted, including the F-111 piece, which set a record at the time of 45,000 copies.

I also rode along with the legendary air show performer Bob Hoover, in his Rockwell twin-engine Shrike Commander, observing him perform his signature engine-out loop to an eight-point roll and single-wheel touchdowns before landing. Watching Hoover at work in the cockpit reminded me of a symphony orchestra's conductor since he seemed synchronized with the machine we were flying.

Being present at the unveiling of new aircraft designs and observing first flights also was a basic and rewarding part of my reporting job. This put me on the front line of the latest technology in the aviation world and provided continuing education and an opportunity to meet and become friends with some of the top pilots, engineers and managers in the US aviation industry.

My general area of responsibility ranged up and down the West Coast from San Diego to Seattle. It included air force and NASA test operations at Edwards AFB and firms involved in the military, space and commercial businesses.

Among the more exciting and challenging were the rollout and first flight of the USAF/North American XB-70A Mach 3 intercontinental bomber and the unveiling of the USAF/Lockheed Mach 3 YF-12A. Both had tight secrecy boundaries on releasable information, which required lots of estimating on performance and flight regime capabilities based partially on studying photos taken at the scene of the rollout or first flight.

McGraw-Hill was so impressed with my reporting activities that they featured me in an ad illustrated by a photo showing me climbing a ladder and peering into the cavernous rear enclosure of the six-engine XB-70A during its rollout.

I also wrote about and observed various flights of the HL-10 and M2 lifting body research aircraft at NASA Flight Research Center and was present at Edwards AFB when the Ryan XV-5A prototype V/STOL aircraft crashed, killing the pilot.

Design stories and first flights of the Douglas DC-9 and DC-10 and the Boeing 727 and 747 were completed, as were in-depth reports on the designs of both the Boeing and Lockheed Supersonic Transport configurations.

At Palmdale, California, I watched Darryl Greenamyer break the world propeller land speed record in a modified Grumman F-8 Bearcat (originally set in 1937 by a German ME109). Also, I interviewed the Air Force flight crews of the supersonic YF-12A, which set new world speed and altitude records. I wrote the first in-depth pieces about the Hiller OH-5A and Hughes OH-6A light observation helicopters for the Army competition. I also learned to fly the OH-6A well enough to achieve a hover, courtesy of the Hughes Tool Co. chief pilot.

Also covered were new helicopter developments on the West Coast, such as the Lockheed rigid rotor prototype, the Hughes hot-cycle research helicopter, and the Boeing AH-64 attack helicopter, which later became an essential part of army aviation troop support.

Detailing the types of stories that I did clearly establishes the lack of any connection between my reserve flying and the reporting I did for the magazine. Although this seemed obvious at the time, it never seemed to occur to those who continued to suspect that I was using my reserve status and secret clearance as an illegal back door to the classified world.

4

Becoming a combat correspondent in Vietnam

In the summer of 1965, I received a call from Bob Hotz, who wanted to know if I would like to go to Vietnam, and I immediately responded positively. The magazine had sent two editors there previously, Mike Yaffee and Cecil Brownlow, when US policy was governed by the 1954 Geneva Accords, which limited the introduction of new bases and new types of aircraft and weapons.

At that time, the official policy of the United States was to support its ally, South Vietnam, and not to play an independent role in the conflict. Following the Tonkin Gulf episode in August 1964, the policy changed in the following spring of 1965 when President Johnson allowed US forces to fight independently under the local control of the US Military Assistance Command Vietnam (MACV). However, the air war over North Vietnam was tightly controlled at the White House level by President Johnson and his staff throughout his presidency. At the same time, aviation assets in the South were generally left up to MACV to handle.

After settling passport, visa and travel arrangements with Pan Am and getting briefed by Hotz to make sure I had enough alcohol in my system to kill the foreign bugs, I routed through Guam so that I could go to Anderson AFB. This was the home of the large USAF/Boeing B-52 bombers that, at the time, were providing a powerful tool to those in charge of the air war in South Vietnam.

The first story that appeared in the magazine was of the large, lumbering bombers, each dropping sticks of fifty-one 750-lb bombs (carried internally and under the wing) on the humid, suspected jungle hideouts. I watched some of the bombers returning from Vietnam facing their final challenge of the mission, the tricky landing on the B-52s' bicycle landing gear. I also interviewed flight crews at Anderson about these missions.

A reporter from the *Baltimore Sun* on his way to Vietnam happened to be in Guam at the same time. He and I were invited by the governor of Guam to dinner one night—a very fancy affair.

I arrived at Tan Son Nhut air base in Saigon on October 21, 1965, caught a cab to downtown and checked in to the Astor Hotel, where I learned that I could stay only a limited time, so I moved to the ground floor of the Mondial Hotel. Several weeks later, my windows caved in due to a nearby Viet Cong bombing. Repairs were slow to come, making me a bit jittery, so I moved to an upper room.

After arriving, I visited MACV to take care of all the paperwork and familiarization briefings and become a card-carrying reporter both under US and South Vietnamese credentials.

By the fall of 1965, a massive buildup of US forces was underway. This included all of the infrastructure needed to run such a huge operation, including beefed-up public relations departments of all the participating elements, which worked well for the reporting I was doing.

Thus, the starting point of each story began with the appropriate PAO (public affairs officer). If I wanted to see how the 1st Cavalry Division (airmobile) was doing, an army PAO was contacted; for B-52s, it was USAF, and to go on board a carrier, it was Navy. The

Saigon-based PAOs did not accompany me into the field, but they let each command know that I was coming, and they assigned escorts to me. Getting to the destinations in the field was by military air using my MACV reporter card and a set of orders which allowed me to travel space available on any military transport vehicle that had room for me. Air travel was key since the roads were too risky. I used many types of fixed- and rotary-wing military aircraft for moving around the country.

Military Assistance Command, Vietnam, was run by the army under a four-star general (Westmoreland at the time), with the chain of command funneling from MACV through CINCPAC in Hawaii to the Defense Department. At the same time, the State Department maintained an embassy and an ambassador in the country that, along with MACV, dealt with the US's ally, the South Vietnamese government.

The State Department played a significant role in setting news policy and dealing directly with the news media. The Johnson administration often was unhappy with the news that came out of Vietnam in the early '60s, particularly when it was negative, contradicted his policies or revealed information that the administration wanted to keep quiet, and, thus, was the subject of many investigations and studies on how to improve it.

William M. Hammond carefully chronicled this in a book titled *Public Affairs: The Military and the Media 1962–1968*. It describes how, in 1964, the Johnson administration made some significant changes to the organization that dealt with the media to improve news coverage favorability. They approved an army-run MACV Office of Information and made Barry Zorthian the US mission's minister-counselor for public affairs, reporting to the ambassador.

Zorthian, sometimes referred to as the "Czar of News," authored guidance papers on Release of Air Strike Information and Release of Combat Information, which was provided to reporters during MACV accreditation with a request to comply with them voluntarily.

The army was responsible for handling the news media in-country and provided reporters with a MACV accreditation card issued by the MACV Information Office. Another press card was issued separately by the South Vietnamese government. Both cards identified the reporter and the news organization they represented. They also ran daily briefings in Saigon, which included information officers of all the participating services and provided a focal point for releasing all news.

I attempted to meet with Zorthian to understand both documents better, but when he learned the reason for my request, he referred me to a MACV army Lt. Col. Biandi. I spent time with him going over the voluntary guidelines in detail to make sure that I lived within them in my reporting.

At no time did I hear from MACV or the embassy regarding my articles. The navy, which was, in a sense, subordinate to the army/embassy group in handling the news in Vietnam, was the only one that tried to twist the MACV regulations out of context to build a case against me. The fact that the people in charge of handling the news people in Vietnam and had formulated the MACV directives were silent on the matter, points to the navy as a significant nemesis (besides the Johnson-McNamara team).

More positive input came from a member of the Air Force information team who said that during the investigation of my case in Vietnam, he had shown the articles to a high-level general officer in the Air Force and received this reply: "We're clean." This was particularly meaningful given the general's high-level responsibilities.

To become outfitted adequately for my upcoming visits to the field, I visited a black market site where I was surprised by the extensive amount of US military gear which somehow had gotten into the hands of the shadowy purveyors. I bought a pair of jungle boots, green uniform pants, a shirt and a poncho, the latter serving me well in the rainy South Vietnamese climate.

I spent the bulk of my time in the country gathering information, which meant interviewing members of the various services about the specific stories I was pursuing. It would have been convenient to play up my background as a Marine Reserve flyer current in A-4 aircraft to ingratiate myself to the sources I spoke with. However, this approach was so uncomfortable and seemed so dishonest that I carefully avoided this tactic. I rarely talked about my flying background except on specific occasions when flying on missions was discussed, and things like being current in the pressure chamber came up (I was current at the time). The rest of the time, I was just Tony Plattner, *Aviation Week* engineering editor here in Vietnam, to write about the air war, and I did not want to receive any classified briefings.

Being a passenger on an aircraft destined for a strike mission required the crew to sit through a pre-brief covering the basics of communication, intelligence, tactics, the enemy situation and the like. When parts of this information, such as communications frequencies and enemy locations were described as classified, I normally excused myself from these short routines.

I attended the daily MACV press briefings (known as the 5 o'clock follies) whenever I was in Saigon. I found them to be an honest effort to present the ongoing war news to a large cadre from various news organizations, including electronic and print media, despite the demeaning nickname.

The briefers and guests, such as the combatants in the air or on the ground, often provided bits of information that I needed to fill in a story, such as the surface-to-air missiles (SAMs) that I was working on. However, the type of *Aviation Week* stories that I sought required me to go out into the field and observe and speak with those participating directly in the war, so I was not often in Saigon.

My first story about the B-52s, under direction from the magazine, was done in Saigon and filed in the old-fashioned way first by
writing it out by hand and then typing it up on my portable typewriter. Then the manuscript was taken to the telex office in downtown
Saigon, where it was retyped and transmitted to New York. This was
time-consuming. I soon decided my planned two-month tour would
be best used to gather information and write the stories after returning
to Los Angeles, where I could rely on the McGraw-Hill facilities to
pump my stories to the editors in the east.

The B-52 story involved flying in the backseat of an air force F-100
alongside the flotilla of bombers from Anderson AFB at an altitude of
22,000 ft. and observing the large sticks of 750-lb. bombs left over
from World War II cascade down from each aircraft on suspected
underground hideouts. Every time a bomb hit, they destroyed large
patches of jungle and occasionally water buffalos or other animals.
The bombs were dropped in parallel columns to carpet the target area
in an efficient pattern, using radar for positioning. Each explosion was
marked by a large blast pattern in the humid air of the jungle, and it
was hard to believe that any underground tunnel fortifications could
have survived this destructive attack.

Following the F-100 ride, my assigned pilot and I climbed into a
Cessna O-1E forward air control (FAC) plane and flew over the cavernous craters on a battlefield damage assessment and discovered
many remnants of underground fortifications. As we flew close to the
site that had been bombed, a small-arms shot from a nearby survivor
of the carnage came close enough to our light plane for the sonic
shock wave to be heard—a reminder that war was, indeed, taking
place below.

With the first story behind me and with only two months total
time in the country, I turned to a more efficient mode of reporting
and dropped the approach of filing from Saigon. I started accumulat-
ing information that I could put into story form back in Los Angeles.

This included visits to and gaining information about An Khe in the Central Highlands and the 1st Cavalry Division (airmobile), the aircraft carrier *Kitty Hawk* (then on Dixie Station providing support to South Vietnam), marine aviation at Chu Lai and Danang air bases, army Mohawk operations at Vung Tao, Vietnamese and air force operations at Bien Hoa, the Northrup F-5 flight evaluation at Bien Hoa, air force operations at the new air base at Cam Ranh Bay, the control of air support by forward air controllers (FACs), logistics headaches of the war, the impact of the monsoons on air support and a story about the USAF F-105 and its role in the war in the North.

Part of the information-gathering process was to ride along as an observer in various aircraft. In total, including for the B-52 story, I rode on and then reported on the following combat missions:

1. Oct. 25—USAF F-100F two-place jet fighter launched from Tan Son Nhut air base to observe a B-52 strike from the air; no ordnance was expended.
2. Oct. 25—USAF O-1F light forward air control (FAC) aircraft launched from Tan Son Nhut to conduct visual battlefield reconnaissance of the area bombed by the B-52s.
3. Oct. 30—USAF A-1E Skyraider close support propeller-driven aircraft launched from Bien Hoa air base on a prebriefed target, then diverted to a hot target Viet Cong village; white phosphorous and other bombs, as well as napalm, were dropped.
4. Nov. 4—Army UH-1D helicopter launched at first light from First Cavalry Division (airmobile) Catecka Airfield into a hot LZ (landing zone) during the battle of Ia Drang Valley (there were numerous other helicopter missions with the First Cav).
5. Nov. 13—USAF F-4C fighter-bomber launched from Cam Ranh Bay Airfield on a prebriefed strike against suspected VC concentration; rockets and 20 mm ammunition expended from the gun pod.

6. Nov. 20—USMC F-4B fighter-bomber launched from Danang air base on a prebriefed mission, then diverted to strike a hot VC area; bombs and rockets expended.
7. Nov. 27—Army OV-1A twin-turboprop aircraft launched from Vung Tao air base on its first visual reconnaissance mission over the delta in South Vietnam.
8. Nov. 27—Army OV-1A second mission over the delta after landing and refueling.
9. Dec. 1—Navy F-4G fighter-bomber launched from the *Kitty Hawk* aircraft carrier on a prebriefed strike mission against suspected VC concentration; bombs expended.

For photos, I relied on what was available from each service with an emphasis on being the latest available images. I also carried my camera, a Kodak Retina 3C, which I used frequently. I turned over the many rolls of film to *Aviation Week* after returning to the States. Among the many photos of mine used in the magazine was a cover picture of a 105 mm howitzer being unloaded from a Chinook helicopter I rode on and jumped off to get the photo. The howitzer provided support for a 1st Cavalry Division (airmobile) operation in the Central Highlands.

When the air force arranged for a USAF/Douglas Skyraider mission from Bien Hoa, I hired a photographer, and he rode in one of the side-by-side two-seat A-1Es in the four airplane flight. As luck would have it, we were diverted from a preplanned strike onto a hot Viet Cong village target, and he got some spectacular pictures of napalm and white phosphorous bombs being dropped. One of these color photos made the magazine cover and was used as a cover for the 105-page reprint issue, which was a collection of all fourteen of my stories. It sold out quickly after being printed at the end of my series.

Boarding an F-4 Phantom in Vietnam as a reporter for Aviation Week & Space Technology in the fall of 1965. This was one of nine combat missions flown as an observer in different types of aircraft.

The initial story in my Vietnam series was about Boeing B-52 bombers. To observe their bomb drop, I flew alongside a group of B-52s in the rear seat of an F-100, then did a mission in a Cessna O-1 to survey the damage.

February 21, 1966

75 cents

A McGraw-Hill
Publication

Aviation Week awarded me a mounted placard of the cover picture used on the re-print of my fourteen-part series that ran weekly for three months. This shows A-1Es dropping napalm and white phosphorous.

Each of the military aviation services had its own stories with underlying interservice competitions that were part of the inter-service roles and missions squabbles taking place . The Air Force and Navy engaged in an ongoing contest of sortie and ordnance tonnage records. The Marine Corps wanted to maintain responsibility for control of its own aircraft, while the Air Force wanted to have them under their operational network. The Army was flying armed fixed-wing aircraft (OV-1As). The Air Force was worried that this encroached on its mission. I matter-of-factly covered these issues in my stories, declining to escalate them to a level of sensational importance.

When I would return to Saigon, it was often to fill in details or to talk with key individuals who were stationed there about stories such as the Republic F-105 or to line up an interview with the then current premier, Nguyen Cao Ky. Lining up an opportunity to see Ky turned out to be one of the most challenging meetings to coordinate, but I was persistent. I finally met with him for a short period and fired many questions at him. Before becoming premier, he had headed up the Vietnamese air force, so he was very conversant with the aviation aspects of the war and graciously provided answers. He liked the use of B-52s and having access to his own jet-powered F-5 aircraft in addition to the A-1E Skyraiders.

In preparing for this story, I read a book, *Special Agent, Vietnam: A Naval Intelligence Memoir,* written by Douglass H. Hubbard Jr. of the Office of Naval Intelligence's Naval Investigative Service (NIS). During the war, they had offices in Danang and Saigon while I was in the country, but I was never aware of their presence. However, after my stories started appearing in the magazine in early 1966, they would likely have been scrambled in the very intense investigation that took place in the country trying to gather evidence for future prosecution by digging into my reporting activities, such as where I went, who I spoke with and what was discussed.

Most of the work that author Hubbard describes dealt with

criminal activity among sailors and marines serving in Vietnam, such as sabotage, black marketing, drug trafficking, rape, murder and counterespionage. In moving around the country, the agents faced many of the same risks and hardships as military forces. Thus, it is hard to understand the secretive position the navy took in refusing to confirm or deny the existence of all the photographs and documents that the author had submitted.

In trying to figure out what to report on, I was left pretty much on my own but with some limited direction from the magazine. The B-52, 1st Cav, F-105, and SAM stories and an interview with Premier Ky were targeted explicitly by Hotz. Working on the aviation elements of the war was, of course, my focus, so with only two months there, I couldn't spend time going into the field where the ground warriors directly faced the Viet Cong and North Vietnamese enemy. The only exception to this was covering the 1st Cavalry Division (airmobile).

5

Writing the Vietnam Series for *Aviation Week & Space Technology*

After finishing my tour and returning to work in Los Angeles, Hotz and Gregory immediately leaned on me to provide them with a complete list of stories that I planned to write. Thus began the toughest part of the assignment, putting together a series of compelling *Aviation Week*-caliber stories based on two months of vacuuming up information in country.

The job was made much more difficult because I couldn't follow up with sources I spoke with in the field to check details or update things since there was no viable civilian phone link between Los Angeles and military offices in South Vietnam.

My focus as a reporter was to paint as accurate a picture of the subject as possible without biasing the coverage in one direction or another. As a truth seeker, I wanted to spell out what was happening in whatever subject I addressed. Agenda-driven reporting, which seemed to be practiced by some media at the time, held no appeal for me, nor would it have been allowed by the magazine.

On a personal level, I found the antiwar agenda distasteful—it was already starting to brew at the time. I felt strongly that our military forces in the field were doing the job they were ordered to do, and many paid a heavy price. In addition to those who fell on the battlefield, others came home with lingering mental or physical wounds, and protesters vilified many of them.

In approaching the process of putting into words my tour in Vietnam, I followed my standard guidelines of telling-it-like-it-was with the goal of getting as close to the truth as possible. The MACV guidelines laid down by the State Department for covering the war at the time allowed reporters access to military operations and let them describe what they were able to observe personally. Reporters were only allowed access to combat operations in South Vietnam and were not permitted to ride on missions to the North.

Military censorship as practiced in previous US conflicts had been considered. It was rejected for numerous reasons, not the least of which was due to the nature of the US participation as a supporting ally of the South Vietnamese and the complications of trying to fashion a tight control of the news under an arrangement involving South Vietnam and the US chain of command.

Some in the chain of command, such as General Westmoreland, favored censorship, but after many discussions of the issue, it was finally decided to proceed without it.

Censorship of mail and news media organizations had some history dating to the Revolutionary and Civil Wars. However, it became an organized practice in World War I, World War II and Korea. In World War II, the news media's censorship was voluntary under a set of guidelines issued by the Office of Censorship that reported directly to Commander in Chief Roosevelt. The system in World War II was based on the cooperation of the newspapers and radio stations who would clear any questionable material with assigned censors in advance of publication or broadcast. Generally, the system worked quite well, with the censor having the final say.

In Vietnam, reporters' cooperation was requested under

self-censorship guidelines issued to them when they became credentialed. These guidelines requested the withholding of timely information on battlefield operations that would give the enemy an advantage once reported. Since none of my reporting was up-to-the-minute, this concern over giving away real-time information to the enemy was not relevant. However, I did practice some self-censorship on such things as tactics that I thought could be useful to the communists in the North and South.

My penchant for accuracy, which had been drilled into me, required careful logging of details during the digging process in the field. For this, I wrote down everything longhand and filled up over six spiral-bound 5½-by-8½ notebooks consisting of 900 pages of notes. These, of course, contained names of sources and topics at all the sites I visited, so I guarded them closely.

With the B-52 story behind me—it appeared Nov. 29, 1965—I focused on the kickoff story for the rest of the series, which began in the Jan. 3, 1966, issue. Hotz introduced the series with a full-page editorial titled "THE LONG WAR," which, in part, painted a picture of my qualifications for covering the war. The editorial, in part, read:

"The series that begins in this issue on p. 16 is the result of two months of travel in Southeast Asia by C. M. (Tony) Plattner, a member of this magazine's Los Angeles Bureau who has an unusual set of qualifications for this task.

"'Tony' Plattner served four years active duty as a Marine Corps fighter pilot flying Vought Corsairs and Grumman F9F-5s and is now a captain in the Marine Air Reserve flying Douglas A-4E jet attack aircraft. His 2,000 hr. of flying time also include many pilot report assignments for AW&ST in a wide variety of aircraft. His latest, before leaving for Vietnam last fall, was a chock-to-chock exercise in the left-hand seat of the Douglas DC-9 (AW&ST, Nov. 1, p. 37). He was educated as a mathematician and worked as an engineer in the aerospace industry and as a newspaper reporter before joining this magazine three years ago.

"During his two months in Southeast Asia, he covered every form of air operation from the Strategic Air Command Boeing B-52 strike based in Guam to the Cessna O-1E light plane spotter missions. He traveled over 1,500 mi. in the combat theater visiting USAF, Army and Marine squadrons and flew combat missions (see photo below of him climbing into an F-4) as an observer in three types of McDonnel Phantom 2 strike fighters, a Bell UH-1D helicopter, a North American F-100 and a Grumman OV-1A Mohawk Army reconnaissance aircraft. He also went on board navy carriers operating off the Vietnam coast to report on the operations."

Aside from a couple of minor technical glitches—I had never flown the Corsair, and the current model of the A-4 that I was flying was not the latest E model but the old As and Bs—I was flattered by the high praise. Although it was not immediately apparent, the editorial detailing my reserve status probably was like waving a red flag at a "bull," inviting retaliation by the Defense establishment and, more particularly, by the navy.

My kickoff story running a lengthy six book pages—I was never known for my brevity—in the same Jan. 3 issue was titled "Force Buildup Keyed to Wider Escalation" by C. M. Plattner and included these points:

- "Despite the rapid acceleration of the US effort since mid-July, there has been no significant change in the military balance between the opposing sides."
- "The rate of infiltration of supplies and men into South Vietnam from the North has increased. The White House-controlled strikes . . . in North Vietnam also have failed in the secondary goal to try to discourage the Hanoi government from continued aggression."
- Pilots believe that mining Haiphong Harbor should be done to cut off supplies at the source. Most military officials here

would like to have the White House wraps removed from other tactical targets in Vietnam, including dams, chemical plants and other industrial complexes in order to cripple the country's productive capacity."

- "Without a series of decisive, crippling victories over the Viet Cong, there appears to be no short-term solution to the problem of winning the war in Vietnam in the conventional sense. Some officials here still feel that a nonnuclear approach to victory could take as long as ten years."

A major story then appeared every week except Mar. 7 and 28, ending with the fourteenth story on Apr. 11, 1966.

On Feb. 21, a story titled "Viet Sorties Rate Pressed as Political Purpose Fails" by C. M. Plattner began:

"Saigon—White House-directed air strikes against North Vietnam are 87 percent political and 13 percent military, a high-ranking USAF official said here. He adds that "our effort up there is peanuts compared with what we should be doing. All we've done so far is force them to tighten their belts a little and work a little harder to move the supplies, but we haven't really hurt them.

"The political goal of the strikes over North Vietnam recently resumed after a 37-day pause (AW&ST, Feb. 7, p. 22) is to discourage Hanoi from further aggression in the South by interdicting and destroying major lines of communications with an occasional attack against harder targets such as a power plant.

"The goal has not been achieved . . ."

The Jan. 3 and Feb. 21 stories included hard-hitting truths of the limited progress in the conflict, particularly the air war. Through later research, a great deal of the information included in my stories was found in the Pentagon Papers, which, at the time, were highly classified documents. Of course, I had no access to information known to be classified at the time. Still, I mention this as a verification of my reporting accuracy from what always was prefaced as unclassified interviews.

The one thing that came through loud and clear in discussions with those conducting the air war up North was the level of frustration among those who put their life on the line every day. Many would eventually spend time in the Hanoi prison camps. Their unhappiness stemmed from President Johnson's political approach as commander in chief to running the air war. His dainty strategic persuasion philosophy and tit-for-tat gambits in the air war, with on-again, off-again bombing halts and general reluctance to put some strong hurt on the North, never brought the North Vietnamese to seriously enter negotiations to end the war during his tenure as commander in chief.

Many histories of the handling of the war by Johnson and his Defense Secretary Robert McNamara note that Johnson took a hardline position against mining the North's harbors to shut off the flow of supplies and handpicked targets in the belief that it would prevent Chinese ground troops from entering the war against US forces, as happened in Korea. He also for several years excluded the military from the top-level decision-making meetings of his civilian advisors, where they discussed bombing targets and strategies.

Johnson's successor, President Richard Nixon, and his security advisor, Henry Kissinger, later disregarded Johnson's concerns and not only bottled up shipping in the harbors with mines but unleashed the terrifying B-52s over Hanoi and Haiphong.

After my stories started appearing in the magazine, a very positive reaction occurred, with many commenting on my reporting's excellent quality. *Aviation Week*'s editor in chief, Bob Hotz, summed up the feedback in a June 28, 1966, memo to me this way:

"Now that most of the returns are in, and you have had a chance to rest and recuperate, I want to let you know that your Viet Nam series was one of the finest editorial jobs this magazine has ever done. The impact has been terrific and genuine. The accuracy has been as

close to 100 percent as is humanly possible. With all of the intensive readership this series has generated, I have received less than half a dozen complaints on accuracy, of which less than half were justified, and they were all in the minor nitpicking category. On the positive side, the reaction has been tremendous with 'the best material I have read on Viet Nam,' an almost standard comment.

"Top-level McGraw-Hill management has also been impressed. President Joe Allen cited our reprint of your series to the managing editors meeting last month as an example of what the corporation's magazines should do more of. We certainly threw you into the deep water with that Pan Am ticket to Saigon, but you certainly showed us you could swim Olympic style."

Some of the other comments included:

- Minnesota Congressional Representative Odin Langen read into the Congressional Record Feb. 28, 1966, my SAM article and accompanied it with high praise for the series (he represented the district including my hometown of Walker, Minnesota).
- Herb Coleman of the magazine's London Bureau wrote, "I thought you'd like to know that the new British Minister of Aviation (Fred Mulley) thinks your coverage of Vietnam is the best he's seen. So do I."
- David Anderton, the magazine's respected technology editor, wrote, "Your report on the B-52 bombing raid in Vietnam is the best single piece of military reporting I have yet seen from that tortured country. There was more new and different information in that one piece than in all the material run previously in *Aviation Week*."
- Harry Kolcum of the magazine's Washington Bureau said the commandant of the Marine Corps' aide called the office and reported that "the Feb. 14 story on Marine Aviation was

great. He is making it required reading for the top 100 USMC generals."

Unfortunately, there was no opportunity of acclaim for the series since *Aviation Week,* at that time, did not believe in entering journalism award contests following in the path of other media giants like *Time* magazine.

6

The ONI "gumshoes" call again, and I lose my flying status in the reserves

Not everyone found my reporting praiseworthy. Unknown to me at the time, an investigation of serious proportions was underway in the Defense Department over the issue of printing classified information in some of my Viet Nam articles, with the navy leading the charge as they had with my A-2F story. After finishing my Vietnam series in April, I continued with my normal reporting activities and flying as a weekend warrior in the reserves. Then on Oct. 8, 1966, I received another surprise visit from the ONI agents.

The two agents, A. R. Arrigo and S. B. Chenowith, had come to my house in Rowland Heights, California, on a Saturday and asked my wife to see me saying they needed to speak with me about my commission. I had gone to Lockheed Aircraft's facility at Rye Canyon to fly their supersonic transport simulator and, following that, to their Burbank plant to finish the engineering briefing on their SST design. When Helen told them I had gone to fly a supersonic transport, they asked if I had flown a military airplane there, and she said that I had driven my car. Being patient detectives, they finally tracked me down in the Lockheed-Burbank parking lot around 6:00 p.m.

After greeting me like an old friend, Arrigo and I talked for a period with me trying to find out what in the world was going on, and he trying to coax me into a private interview in his office. I did learn that they were investigating my Vietnam series and that they would like to meet privately so phone calls could be made to Washington, D.C., where my officer's jacket was maintained. The discussion on my commission was a strange twist in this developing investigation. At first blush, it was hard to get my arms around the true seriousness of the situation.

My meeting with Arrigo several years earlier on my A-2F story provided a hint at the nature of their visit, which likely had to do with publishing so-called classified information. However, up to this point, the very limited indication from these conversations gave only an ominous hint that something big was taking place behind the secrecy curtain. The true nature of the massive effort underway to prosecute me would only come into focus years later after a dogged pursuit on my part to peel back the onion, layer by layer, to gain a clear understanding of why DOD was pursuing me.

Since I was in the information-gathering mode, particularly on the matter of my jacket, I thought that a meeting in Arrigo's office might shed some light on this issue and tentatively agreed to meet with him.

I said I would call him back, and on Oct. 10, after bringing up the matter with the management of *Aviation Week,* I informed him that if he wanted to discuss my role as a civilian reporter for *Aviation Week,* it would have to take place in the magazine's Los Angeles office in the presence of a witness and that if he wanted to discuss my military status, it should be done through military channels. Agent Arrigo, undoubtedly disappointed at the response to his back-door query, never set a future meeting with me.

Following the ONI visit, I fired off a bold, lawyerlike letter to the commandant on Oct. 30, 1966, describing the parking lot meeting. I asked that . . . "any official comment made by or document received from any agency of the government that could in any way be considered detrimental to me in my military capacity be referred to me for rebuttal. In this way, it will be possible for me to prevent the planting of a seed of doubt of my loyalty and discretion based on mistaken perception. I wish to emphasize that this letter is in regard to my status as an officer of the Marine Corps Reserve and does not concern any investigation of *Aviation Week* or its staff."

Three months later, on Feb. 8, 1967, I received a phone call from Headquarters, Marine Corps notifying me that I was being transferred from active Class II flying status to Class III individual ready reserve status. This was followed by a set of orders directing the transfer. Although not spelled out in the phone conversation or in the set of orders, there was an additional behind-the-scenes directive to the Marine Air Reserve Training detachment to suspend my access to classified information.

It turned out that the directive to deny me access to classified information had, unbeknownst to me, actually taken place in October. However, since nothing was classified about flying the A-4, I kept on flying until the February 8 phone call.

Although I was vaguely aware that ONI was investigating my Vietnam reporting from the agents' visit the previous fall, losing my flying status came as a heavy blow. Because there was no explanation for the action taken and spurred by the directive's perceived injustice, I set about strategizing on coping with the situation, using whatever resources that I could muster.

The first avenue of pursuit was through the military chain of command, although I held out little hope for any success on this route. After determining that the commanding general of the 4th Marine Air Wing (the Reserve Wing of the Marine Corps) saw no use in talking to me, I fired off a letter to the Marine Corps' Commandant requesting mast on Feb. 16, 1967. On March 22, I sent the commandant another letter asking him to reply to my previous letters.

On Mar. 31, he replied to my mast request, saying, "all aspects of your case are known and have been reviewed by the Commandant. Accordingly, your appearance at this Headquarters would serve no useful purpose, and your request for mast is denied." The letter was signed by L. F. Chapman, Jr., Chief of Staff.

Then on Apr. 23, 1967, another CMC letter arrived, replying to my October request (five and a half months previous) for an opportunity of rebuttal. It said, "Current regulations on the releaseability of investigative files and the still pending status of your case preclude granting the request contained in your October letter. It should be noted that the transfer to Class III status was an interim measure pending final resolution of your case."

The letter did nothing to clarify what the "case" against me meant or how much trouble it portended. But it left little doubt in my mind that it reflected a serious, highly secretive investigation taking place somewhere inside the Defense Department.

Since I was no longer a member of the VMA-241 Reserve Squadron at NAS, Los Alamitos, I checked out and temporarily stopped active participation in the Marine Reserve and, of course, continued my reporting job at *Aviation Week*. With a resolution of my case dead-ended via the military chain of command, I turned to civil resources.

7

I look to Congress for help

I contacted my congressman, Charles E. Wiggins (California 24th District). I followed it up with a lengthy letter on July 27, 1967, tracing the history of my case, which ended with being booted out of the Reserve with no charges and no explanation. I also believed that this was a retaliatory measure for doing a good reporting job on the Vietnam War.

I described the stone-walling of my efforts to learn about my case through the Marine Corps and noted that it was a year and a half since my Vietnam series began in *Aviation Week*. My long-range goal, I told him, was to confront any charges, set the record straight and return to flying status.

Wiggins was very sympathetic and made a phone call on August 22, 1967, to then commandant of the Marine Corps, Wallace M. Greene, Jr., asking for a status report on my case. Commandant Greene replied shortly to Wiggins in a lengthy letter dated August 25, 1967, providing, for the first time, a good outline of the case against me. The letter read, in part:

"The pending action in the case of Major Plattner concerns the articles he wrote for Aviation Week & Space Technology *magazine in early 1966. Detailed review of these articles has revealed that they contained highly sensitive and critical classified information.*

"Initial action on this matter was taken on 25 February 1966 when the Director for Security Review, Office of the Assistant Secretary of Defense (Public Affairs) referred the case to the Directorate for Inspection Services (DINS). This referral was in accordance with responsibilities of the Directorate for Inspection Services concerning unauthorized disclosures of classified defense information. Subsequently, the matter was investigated by the Directorate for Inspection Services, the Naval Investigative Services, and the Office of Special Investigations, US Air Force.

"Results of these investigations were forwarded to the Federal Bureau of Investigation for an opinion concerning prosecution. Additional information developed by the Directorate for Inspection Services was forwarded to the Assistant Attorney General by the Federal Bureau of Investigation on 5 May 1967. On 1 August 1967, the Department of Justice informed the Federal Bureau of Investigation that the matter was under study and a decision could be expected in the near future.

"Major Plattner's statement regarding his unclassified interviews and access as a Reserve pilot are essential to an understanding of this case. To fly the missions he flew in Vietnam and to carry out his reserve duties as a pilot, Major Plattner necessarily received access to classified information. His military and civilian background, both as a pilot and reporter, permitted him to perceive and understand incidents and trends not readily apparent to other reporters.

"The quality of his reporting cannot be disputed. What can be disputed, however, was the inclusion in his articles of sensitive information, subsequently determined to have been classified, which unquestionably was of material benefit to enemy forces in North Vietnam.

"It is acknowledged that this case has certain sensitive and controversial implications. In recognition of these implications, this Headquarters has acted in such a manner as not to prematurely *prejudice Major Plattner's case. He was not 'summarily kicked out' of the active Reserve, but rather transferred to non-drill pay status by a routine administrative action that would cause no adverse publicity or aftereffects.*

"This action was initiated by the Marine Corps as the means by which to best protect the interests of both the Marine Corps and individual concerned. Further, the Marine Corps refused to judge the case prematurely on the basis of incomplete information and took no action to withhold Major Plattner's promotion to his present rank in 1966. Future Marine Corps actions will necessarily be determined by the results of the Department of Justice review. You may be assured that should the Marine Corps initiate any action as a result of the review, Major Plattner will be informed of the action and afforded every legal right due him."

Copies of the letter also were sent to Senators Kuchel and Murphy and Representatives Langen and Moss. By then, I had enlisted the assistance of my California senators, Thomas H. Kuchel and George Murphy, and California Representative John E. Moss, c hairman of the Foreign Operations and Government Information Subcommittee of the House Committee on Government Operations. My father had taken my case to his Minnesota representative, Odin Langen, who proved very useful in continuing to seek information as the case unraveled.

Commandant Greene's letter lifted the veil of secrecy surrounding my case to a limited degree. It provided for the first time the scope of the government's ferocious effort to prosecute me under the Espionage Act. It also used ominous-sounding language such as "inclusion in his articles of sensitive information subsequently determined to have been classified, which unquestionably was of material benefit to enemy forces in North Vietnam."

If one were to believe the letter's ominous-sounding charges and conclusions, some serious security violations had taken place in my

Vietnam War reporting. However, I absolutely knew that such was not the case. It helped me formulate a future strategic path of setting the record straight to prove my innocence as a competent journalist and a loyal marine reservist.

The letter identified the source and date of the kickoff of the investigation as coming from the Office of the Assistant Secretary of Defense (Public Affairs) on Feb. 25, 1966. The Public Affairs Office, which was responsible for press relations, was run by Arthur Sylvester, who worked directly for Robert McNamara, the Defense Department secretary.

The timing of the initiation of DOD's investigation coincided almost exactly with the publication of my Feb. 21 story titled "Viet Sorties Rates Pressed as Political Purpose Fails." Publishing the lack of progress in the war undoubtedly enraged high-level officials in the Defense Department and/or White House. This became the trigger mechanism, although, as later would become evident, the navy was already working away on its own initiative, trying to gather evidence for a court case against me.

The Office of the Assistant Secretary of Defense (Public Affairs) was run by Arthur Sylvester, a former newspaper reporter who DOD Secretary Robert S. McNamara had selected on Jan. 20, 1961. He served until Feb. 3, 1967, when Phil Goulding succeeded him. There is little doubt that Sylvester was aware of and probably authorized the directive to investigate me. Since he worked directly for McNamara, it is almost certain that his boss would also have been aware of the steps being taken to prosecute a journalist for his Vietnam reporting.

Arthur Sylvester was well known in the fraternity of reporters covering the war in Vietnam for his confrontational attitude toward them. For example, he had accompanied McNamara to Vietnam in mid-July 1965 with the idea of obtaining a more favorable output from the reporters stationed there. William Hammond, in his book *Public Affairs: The Military and the Media 1962–1968,* recounts a so-called bull session in the summer of 1965 with selected journalists, when Sylvester said he failed to understand "how you guys can write what you do while American boys are dying out there." Later, he is recalled as saying, "Look, if you think any American official is going to tell you the truth, you're stupid. In time of war, the news media had the obligation to become the 'handmaiden' of government."

Previously, during the Cuban Missile Crisis in 1962, Sylvester became notable for defending the position of government officials lying to the press in the interest of national security. Sylvester and McNamara were sometimes targets of *Aviation Week*'s editor, Bob Hotz, in his editorials for lying to the American people.

Besides McNamara, President Johnson would likely have been aware of the case against me and even may have played a role in launching the investigation. Both these individuals had strong feelings against what they considered an adversarial press for stories that were not to their liking on Vietnam. Both regularly tried to manage the news media.

Aviation Week was considered the bible of the industry and was renowned for its detailed, inside reporting (sometimes referred to as *Aviation* "Leak"). My dual role as a civilian reporter and a Marine Reserve flyer undoubtedly offered a convenient but completely erroneous handle for the dogged pursuit of my case for those who held a strong antimedia bias.

There was, however, little doubt about the navy's role in all this. They had branded me early on after my A2F story in 1963 as a source for publishing classified information and saw the Vietnam series as verification of this misguided belief. This combination of forces continued to drive my case forward with a strong, unrelenting thrust emanating from the highest levels at the chief of Naval Operations and Defense Department. Although not involved in it early on, the Marine Corps became swept up in this tidal movement.

The Greene letter did have a positive side. It provided me with a base to continue through my congressional ombudsmen to elicit follow-up inquiries on the status of my case since it said that the Defense Department had forwarded the case to the Justice Department.

By late August 1967, there was no indication of the Justice Department's position and renewed inquiry from Senator Murphy to the Justice Department turned up the following information from J. Walter Yeagley, assistant attorney general:

"I have your communication of August 25, 1967, to the Department requesting to be advised as to the final disposition of the matter involving Major Clemens M. Plattner, United States Marine Corps Reserve. As General Greene has noted in his letter to you of August 21, 1967, this case was referred to us by the Department of Defense for prosecutive considerations as a consequence of Defense's determination that Plattner had published classified information in Aviation Week & Space Technology *magazine, without authorization. This information was allegedly gained by Plattner as a correspondent in South Vietnam for the magazine in late 1965.*

"On the basis of the information furnished by the Department of Defense, we have concluded that portions of the information contained in articles authored by Major Plattner were published by him after he was advised by military authorities that for security reasons, such information should not be publicly disclosed. The Department of Defense has advised us, however, that this information is currently classified and cannot be released for prosecutive purposes at this time.

"As you may know, in order to support a prosecution for unauthorized disclosure of national defense information under the provisions of Title 18, United States Code, Section 793, it is necessary to introduce at a public trial and submit to the jury, the information which allegedly relates to the national defense of the United States and which, it is contended, the defendant disclosed without authorization. In view of Department of Defense's determination that the

classified information published by Major Plattner cannot be identi-fied and disclosed publicly, prosecution cannot be undertaken at the time."

This baffling Catch-22 position conveniently bottled up the case at DOJ, leaving me in limbo once more since nothing further could be done until DOD declassified the evidence. This was the first in-kling that the case against me was starting to unravel, but this per-spective only became apparent in hindsight—at the time, no such weakness was obvious.

I shared the results of the congressional inquiries with the maga-zine management, and Hotz invited me back to his Washington, D.C., office to discuss how to deal with the situation. On Nov. 27, 1967, I met with Hotz and Cecil Brownlow in a meeting stretching from 1:30 to 6:30 p.m. before heading to the Press Club bar. Different strategies were mulled over, one of which was to ferret out who was behind the investigation. Nothing much grew out of this effort, which only added to my growing anxiety with the lack of progress in resolving my case.

While in Washington, D.C., the location of Headquarters of the Marine Corps, I went to see my jacket. The officer qualifications jack-ets were kept in paper files and were available for review on-site by the officer in person. After presenting my ID card, I was given my jacket, which I carefully reviewed and copied down the following information:

- Section three—undesirable, disciplinary action, etc.—was completely blank.
- Fitness reports were all above average, generally excellent to outstanding, several particularly desire to have.
- Most frequently used adjectives were: excellent pilot, con-scientious, quiet, intelligent, knowledgeable about aviation, highly recommend retention or promotion, hard worker, does a good job of collateral duties, serious, strong devotion to duty.

This was a good sign and indicated that the Marine Corps had not salted my jacket with negative information. These jackets provide promotion boards with the basic information needed to advance an individual to the next rank or to pass him over. Promotion boards meet annually, and once in the zone, an officer has three years to advance to the next rank or be retired.

By 1968, after stopping my reserve participation the previous February, a good friend of mine, Don Brennan, a marine pilot in World War II, told me about his flying experiences with a local sky-typing outfit. Don was the leading *Aviation Week* advertising salesman on the West Coast and had a long association with an outfit called Stinis Air Service, which had recently brought six of its twelve North American/navy SNJ trainer aircraft from New York to Long Beach in search of less cloudy weather.

He introduced me to the manager, Greg Stinis, the owner's son, and I offered my services as a pilot and was immediately accepted. Besides my reserve flying, I was familiar with the SNJ from the navy flight training program, so I melded right into the operation and be-gan flying next to Brennan on the left side of the five-plane formation (I was known as the "lower puff").

Each of the airplanes was fitted with a tank for the paraffin-based smoke oil in the rear seat (normally where the instructor sat) and a radio that received signals from the lead airplane in the middle of the formation flown by Stinis. His airplane was equipped with a one-of-a-kind player similar to an automatic piano player using a paper roller on which a special typewriter typed the advertising message.

The puffing was done automatically. After my plane received the radio signal to puff from Stinis's airplane in the center of the forma-tion, a solenoid opened to squirt a dollop of smoke oil into the hot engine exhaust vented through a long pipe mounted atop the inboard right wing and exiting over the trailing edge. The pilot's task was to maintain a line-abreast formation with the correct spacing between planes, somewhat simplified by a U-shaped sighting device mounted on the wingtip.

I enjoyed the flying and the camaraderie with a very experienced crew of flyers, including an experimental test pilot and a group of World War II and Korean War aviators, and the happy hour event after each flight at a local bar. Don Brennan and I held down the left side as the marine contingent of the five-airplane formation for about ten years until I moved to Seattle, Washington, in 1979.

During this time, I devoted many of my holidays and weekends to the sky-typers. We often would fly along the Southern California beaches on Saturday morning from San Diego to Santa Barbara, puffing out the message, "TAN DON'T BURN, USE COPPERTONE." Then on Sunday afternoon, we would write, "FOR SUNBURN PAIN USE SOLARCAINE." The same company made both products.

Our flight line was at the Long Beach Airport. Besides flying along the beaches, we were regulars over such events as the Rose Bowl on New Year's Day and special occasions such as the opening of London Bridge at Lake Havasu, Arizona. By flying straight ahead and putting out a dot-matrix message, we could get around twenty-five characters in the sky before the letters started to dissipate as opposed to single-plane skywriting, which generally produced only a few readable characters.

The SNJs were a pretty reliable bunch of birds, but I encountered one memorable problem on takeoff to the west one day with my engine at full throttle when it temporarily stopped. I panicked for a moment since straight ahead was a large collection of fuel storage tanks, so I started a left turn despite the normal advice to fly straight ahead in an emergency. Shortly thereafter, the engine caught again, and I continued a climbing left turn to enter the downwind. I called the tower and reported my problem, and on the downwind leg, the engine stopped again, so I declared an emergency and told the tower I was setting down on the nearest runway, the long, northwest runway.

Again, the engine caught back up after I had landed, and I taxied to the flight line.

After exiting the airplane and conducting the postflight checklist, which included positioning the propeller in a horizontal position, when I started turning it, a loud clunk sounded inside the engine. It froze in position, indicating that some of the internal mechanisms had broken. I was thankful that my old faithful number 6 bird had gotten me safely back on the ground before dying.

The year 1968 was a period of no-news frustration regarding my case since the Justice Department had bottled it up, but I didn't quit worrying about it. By May, frustration had warped my thought processes to the extent that I put together a brash letter to the commandant virtually demanding action on my case and saying that "I would consider immediate unrestricted return to Class II reserve status as an A-4 pilot at Los Alamitos an acceptable solution to the matter. The only other acceptable solution which I now see is for the government to press formal charges against me so that I can defend myself. Be aware that my resolve is steadfast and through whichever means become necessary will be taken to vindicate me."

Those copied were listed as secretary of defense, secretary of the navy, president of McGraw-Hill, *Aviation Week* publisher and editor. I then sent a draft to Hotz for review. Holding up the mailing of the letter while I heard from him was the only sensible decision I made about this head-down charging maneuver. Both Publisher Martin and Editor Hotz counseled strongly against sending the letter and turned my thinking around so that I never sent the letter. Both also talked about how they would continue their efforts to plan a strategy for resolving the matter.

During this time, another tactic that I came up with was to enlist a famous lawyer's assistance, in this case, F. Lee Bailey, a marine pilot. He had an office in a law firm on the West Coast. I tracked him down at a nightclub one evening and put my case to him—one marine aviator to another marine aviator.

By this time, I had honed my message to a pretty persuasive pitch, and Mr. Bailey listened with a sympathetic ear. Of course, I had no idea how I would finance a retainer, but the issue didn't arise at the first encounter.

Lee asked me to come into his office in Beverly Hills the following morning. After providing him with background correspondence via the congressional route, he dictated a letter to the commandant. His letter to Leonard F. Chapman, Jr., dated Aug. 23, 1968, read: *"I have been made aware of correspondence with certain congressmen and representatives. There is a claim that Major Clemens M. Plattner, 062564, printed classified information. As a former Marine Corps aviator, I know how he feels about it, and that it is a blight on his record.*

"I feel that he should be advised what material he printed that was made available to him in the office as a marine reservist."

Bailey put his finger on one of the soft points of the case by asking what information had been available to me as a marine reservist that I printed as classified information. On Aug. 28, 1968, Colonel M. G. Truesdale, Director Judge Advocate Division, replied for the commandant:

"Please be advised that the future status of Major Plattner is still under consideration by this Headquarters. In determining the final action in this matter, Major Plattner will be afforded an opportunity to present any matter to controvert allegations that may be brought against him and to demonstrate his past and future worth as a member of the Marine Corps Reserve.

"As a former Marine pilot, I am sure you can understand the difficult position of the Marine Corps when faced with the question of the possible unauthorized disclosure of classified information on the one hand and the need for qualified pilots on the other. Please be assured that no final action will be taken in this matter without Major Plattner having been afforded all his administrative and legal rights."

This, again, put a lid on any official news on my case. I was deeply appreciative of Mr. Bailey's efforts on my behalf, but there didn't appear to be anything more that he could do until the case matured into a courtroom event.

In the meantime, I held out some hope that following our initial get-together, Hotz and the company would perform some miracle and get the situation resolved. However, seeing the general scope of the case against me provided little hope that the magazine actually could do anything.

I had kept him up to speed with copies of letters obtained by the congressmen, and on September 19, 1967, I wrote him a memo suggesting that we seek legal counsel from the magazine's parent, McGraw-Hill. In the memo, I also recalled a recent meeting in Seattle in which he indicated that he didn't plan to do anything else, so I said that I would assume that this philosophy would continue to prevail. There was never a reply to my suggestion of getting McGraw-Hill lawyers involved.

Using the congressmen without consulting him had put Hotz in a negative mood. In early 1969 when I said that I planned to write a letter to the Justice Department to check on my case, he wrote back that this was not a good idea, although this advice turned out to be the opposite of what was needed to get Justice to clarify its position.

Time continued to slip away. I was now flying solo in trying to resolve my case without backing from *Aviation Week*. So on January 6, 1969, I decided to call the Justice Department myself. Then surprisingly, on January 9, 1969, almost two years since being transferred off flying status and three years since my articles were published, I received a call-back from DOJ trial attorney Joseph Eddins. He informed me that the file on my case had been closed in February or March 1968 after deciding against prosecution.

This belated good news meant that Justice had denied the Defense Department's original plans to have me prosecuted in civil court under the Espionage Act. This was heartening, but there still remained the Defense Department to deal with, and I seemed no closer to my goal of setting the record straight and returning to flying status.

8

Breaking the logjam

Coincidentally, an old squadron mate of mine, Steve Sadler, was back in Los Angeles from Vietnam, and we had lunch on that same day— Jan. 9, 1969. I had looked him up when I was in Saigon in the fall of 1965, and we shared some cocktails and dinners whenever I was not in the field. He was on vacation from his job flying Twin Beechcrafts for the CIA's Air America Airline.

He listened to my story with interest and volunteered that he knew President Johnson's Marine Corps aide from basic school and suggested we call him. We did just that the same afternoon. Steve introduced me, and I followed with a lengthy explanation of my case. After listening politely, he suggested that I provide him with more details. I immediately pumped out a letter that same day to Col. Haywood R. Smith, Armed Forces Aide, White House, Washington, D.C.

In the January 9, 1969, letter, I said my goal is to return to Class II Marine Corps Air Reserve flying status. I then recapped the frustrations of trying to gain information during the two years since being taken off flying status and capped it off with the latest news that the Justice Department had declined to prosecute my case. I said:

"Some official excuse always has been found to prevent my return to flying status and keep me from presenting my side. I feel that the

Marine Corps basically is a middleman in this mess and that someone in DOD or possibly the navy provided the tenacious forcing function behind it.

"This is not to say I believed everyone in USMC is pro Plattner despite my record which shows I am a good pilot and officer, but I would like the opportunity to present my side so I can persuade the Marine Corps that I should be permitted to return to Class II. I believe DOD must first give the green light for this." A detailed history of my case was included and covered my reporting for *Aviation Week* on the war and the investigation that followed, capped off by the Justice Department's refusal to prosecute the case.

Colonel Smith took the matter to Assistant Secretary of the Navy Charles A. Bowsher. He soon replied to me on Jan. 16, 1969, and said, "Upon inquiry into your situation, I was informed that the Commandant of the Marine Corps is currently reviewing your entire case. I am confident that you will receive every consideration in accordance with existing laws and current regulations."

To make sure that this new avenue did not disappear into the backwater of inaction, I sent off a letter to the commandant on February 6, 1969, referencing Bowsher's letter to me and drawing attention again to the DOJ's refusal to prosecute my case. I said:

"I respectfully urge a decision on this matter at the very earliest date. My case has been 'under review' and fraught with 'sensitivity,' which I never have understood, for two years now. Further delay in grappling with the 'pending' status of my case seems unwarranted.

"My record shows I am a good pilot and a loyal officer. I retain a strong motivation for participating in the active reserve program. It is emphasized, however, that this motivation is in no way inspired by my civilian job.

"If the key element in the decision to return me to Class II becomes the status of my security clearance, it is my understanding that regulations exist whereby an individual is entitled to a hearing *in which he may present his side of the matter. Accordingly, I request that all such rights be granted me should this unlikely and unbelievable contingency arise."*

In the Defense establishment hierarchy, the Secretary of the Navy's office is senior to both the Marine Corps and the navy. It is thus capable of applying downward pressure to both services. This was done by forcing the navy, which had been the active protagonist in my case together with the Marine Corps, which owned me as a marine reservist, to take the next step, which was to provide a hearing that presented the charges against me in an unclassified forum and then allow me to respond to them.

One month later, I received a letter dated March 11, 1969, from the Marine Corps. It said that an administrative discharge board was being convened. Commandant L. F. Chapman, Jr.'s, two-page letter was followed by fourteen pages of attachments titled "SUMMARY OF INFORMATION IN THE CASE OF MAJ. CLEMENS MAESER PLATTNER, USMCR, 062564."

Also attached to the main letter was a formal letter of resignation that I could sign and return. It said in paragraph 1, *"In accordance with reference (a), MARCORPSEPMAN Par. 4002, I hereby tender my resignation from the Marine Corps Reserve. If accepted, I understand that my separation shall be under honorable conditions and that I will be awarded a general discharge certificate."*

A more lengthy paragraph 2 went on to conclude: *"This waiver is made in the interest of expediting ultimate disposition of my case, as I feel that my position in the matter has been made clear, and I have full confidence in the ability and fairness of the officers in higher authority who will act upon my case."*

The language "having confidence in the ability and fairness of the officers in higher authority who will act upon my case" would have provided an immediate red flag in light of the frustrations of fighting my case for years. Also, the option of accepting a general discharge under honorable conditions rather than a straight honorable discharge generally assigned at the end of a veteran's active service was not appealing.

I immediately wrote the commandant that I wanted to have a hearing, ignoring the convenient resignation letter. This, of course, carried the potential downside risk that I could be kicked out of the Marine Reserve, lose my commission and perhaps be tagged with a dishonorable discharge. I also might lose any opportunity for reaching the retirement goal of twenty years with its future benefits (I had only about fourteen years of good service at this point).

But the hearing offered me the long-sought opportunity to tell my side of the story, so I plowed ahead, buoyed with the self-confidence that I could prove my case to the discharge board, especially since DOJ had declined to prosecute.

The commandant's letter finally laid out the case that the government had so laboriously worked on. Miraculously, much of the classified information that was the basis for not moving forward in an open hearing was no longer classified. It provided another strange twist that perhaps the information was not as sensitive as first claimed.

Once my case was dropped in the lap of the Marine Corps, the commandant and his staff had set about making as competent an argument as possible out of a very weak, disorganized and inaccurate case that had floated from the Defense Department to the Justice Department and back. In preparing its letter, the Marine Corps, which was now in league with the navy, had access to a large quantity of investigative files to draw from. But it had no solid baseline to prosecute with, so it used a summary prepared previously by the navy as the foundation of their charges against me.

The actual files resulting from the investigation had been built up in stages following the appearance of my series. I was told by one of the information officers at MACV that after the agents came up with minimal information on their first investigative go-around in Vietnam, they were sent back repeatedly to dig deeper for prosecutable evidence.

When the Justice Department finally made a decision--even with the voluminous files-- they obviously saw a flimsy, weak case that had no chance of success in an open hearing in civil court.

The path ahead dealt with the proposition that being a marine reserve flyer gave me some sort of an inside advantage, including access to classified information, in reporting on aviation news. The lengthy summary attachment, which appeared to have been prepared several years earlier for the civil case being considered by the Justice Department.

No doubt, as a lowly reserve major with bronze oak leaves on my collar, I had annoyed the four-star Marine Corps' Commandant with a barrage of letters as well as inquiries from many congressmen and newsmen, Mr. Bailey and Mr. Browsher. In part, this probably explained the tenacious approach used by the Marine Corps and backed by the navy to establish how I had committed serious breaches of security that were of use to the enemy.

The Corps was fighting with the same aggressive approach that it was famous for on the battlefield. Once given the mission that the high authority had determined that I had published classified information after being told not to, it did its best to prevail against me.

I received feedback later that one of the key staffers who put together the case against me actually believed that I had committed criminal acts. However, almost all of those I spoke privately with in the Marine Corps hierarchy—and there were many—felt strongly that I was getting hosed, and I did nothing wrong.

Now that the stage was set for the next major step in resolving my case, there was serious work to do to ensure that this one-time opportunity to tell my side of the story did not result in disaster.

Ensuring the most effective rebuttal of the case laid out against me suggested that I needed legal assistance. The adage that whosoever chooses to represent himself in court has a fool for a lawyer helped point the way. My brother, John Plattner, County Attorney for Cass County, Minnesota, and an excellent lawyer, counseled in this direction, and I began the search for a defense attorney.

Of course, there was F. Lee Bailey, the renowned defense attorney who had a national reputation for participating in defense of such high-profile cases as O. J. Simpson and army Captain Ernest Medina in his court-martial over the My Lai Massacre during the Vietnam War. He had put his oar in the water in my case with a letter to the commandant without asking for any compensation.

There was little doubt in my mind that Bailey, a brilliant lawyer, would easily tear apart the government's case against me. However, he was located on the East Coast, which would have meant extensive travel, and with a family of five children to support and a very modest reporter's salary of $13,000 a year, I didn't have the financial resources that I assumed would be required to hire Mr. Bailey.

Additionally, the nature of the hearing that was to take place was an administrative discharge board which was to be heard only on the basis of the letter written by the commandant. It was not a court room hearing in which procedures such as cross-examinations and producing witnesses could likely occur. At that time, prior to the hearing, I did not favor publicity, although Bailey might have had an opposite opinion on the matter. For these reasons, I never asked Lee to represent me, although once the hearing was convened, there was a great disappointment on the part of the marine lawyers that they would not get to see him in action.

In my magazine reporting on stories other than the Vietnam War, I had been sued twice for roughly $1 million each for two separate stories I had written. McGraw-Hill, also listed as a defendant, hired a top-notch law firm, Gibson, Dunn and Crutcher in Los Angeles, to handle the cases. Both suits were eventually won. The defense attorney assigned by his firm to handle both lawsuits was Theodore B. Olson, who later became the forty-second solicitor general of the United States. He handled the Bush v. Gore case before the Supreme Court, which resolved the contested 2,000 election in favor of President Bush.

Interestingly, in one of the lawsuits involving the inadequate shot peening of a part that caused a crash of a Los Angeles Airways helicopter that I wrote about, Olson pressured me to publicly identify a source that I described in my article only as an NTSB source. I refused to do so, and he went on to win the case anyway. He later would vigorously defend the rights of journalists not to give up their sources in court cases.

In another instance of probing for my sources, I wrote a story about the crash of one of the three XB-70A aircraft that had many details of the accident. Later, I was visited in the *Aviation Week* Los Angeles office by a congressional investigating committee staff. They wanted to know my sources, which I refused to disclose. This occasion was similar to all the other investigative procedures which sought information about people and places. During my time as a reporter, I never revealed any details on sources and places despite persistent pressure from various investigative agencies.

9

Preparing the defense

By now, it had become clear that based on Hotz's negative reaction to my carrying on the crusade against DOD on my own and the fact that Justice had refused to prosecute the civil case against me as a reporter, that McGraw-Hill's legal assistance would not be available. This left me to deal with the military case on my own. So I pulsed an Orange County lawyer who was a marine reservist about handling my defense.

Frank O'Rourke was a ground officer and a bright guy and had sat in on an administrative discharge board hearing recently, so he knew something about the procedures. He was a lieutenant colonel and had been in aviation for most of his career, and, although not a pilot, he had been close to the subject of supporting and controlling marine airplanes.

Previously, I had spoken to him about my situation, and we talked about the generalities of my rights in the case without discussing dollars. When decision time came on whether to take on my case, he finally said, "if you can come up with $2,000, I will give you a good defense." I agreed, and we began preparing for the hearing, which involved extensive backgrounding of Frank, who knew virtually nothing about the case details.

The hearing was initially scheduled to begin on May 12, 1969, at the El Toro Marine Corps Air Station in Irvine, California. A board consisting of three Marine Reserve colonels from Orange County had been appointed to hear the case.

Frank had a somewhat cavalier attitude about the importance of meeting the scheduled date, and despite my objections, requested delays twice due to conflicts with what he claimed were previously scheduled court dates. The Marine Corps reset the May date to July, which meant that the three board members had to change their plans. Then Frank asked for another delay, and the Marine Corps surprisingly complied with an August 4, 1969, date and notified O'Rourke that the hearing would be held on that date with or without his presence. This seemed to get Frank's attention, and we proceeded to work on the case in earnest.

The presentation of a convincing defense on a subject as shadowy and subjective as classified information required careful planning since we had no visibility on protected information and had to prepare based only on the unclassified world where we lived. We were on the outside while the Marine Corps was on the inside with visibility on both the classified and the unclassified world.

The first meeting with Frank on case preparation was on June 15, 1969, at NAS, Los Alamitos, on his drill weekend. Since I was no longer an active reservist, I had to call Frank from the gate and get permission to enter the facility. This was a broad brush look, and the letters Frank had exchanged with the Marine Corps were discussed, including their refusal to bring a key navy witness to the hearing for cross-examination and dropping my request to have the Marine Corps furnish me a lawyer (they later recanted and provided a captain with a law degree).

This was followed by six intense meetings in his Santa Ana office beginning July 24 and ending on August 1. These meetings only came about after my exasperated demands for Frank's time based on the short time remaining before the August 4 deadline. All lawyers are mindful of the clock since their billing is based on the amount of time they devote to a case. During these meetings, we spent twenty-two hours in discussions, which would have quickly used up the $2,000 I paid him, to say nothing of the five days of the hearing and the extensive correspondence exchange with the Marine Corps. Hence, Frank contributed measurably in terms of pro bono work to my defense.

Because of my penchant for accuracy and detail, Frank often became frustrated with our progress, but I give him credit for hanging in there till he absorbed every detail. We got to the point where we felt we had rebutted all of the accusations, and it was apparent that he was prepared to face the board the following Monday.

There were additional elements that we worked on in advance of the August 4 start date. A request had been made of the Marine Corps by me to assign Col. Charles B. Sevier, a competent regular marine lawyer, as my counsel as well as to provide a verbatim record of the proceedings. Both requests were turned down. Initially, a Captain Golden had been assigned to my case, but he was no longer available when his tour was up in July. Then another legal counsel, Captain Campbell, was assigned.

Frank immediately assigned Campbell the task of researching the applicability of the naval regulation 1252 to reservists who worked as journalists.

My brother, John Plattner, already had devoted substantial time and effort to the rights of the accused in administration discharge hearings and furnished several pages of excellent legal research, including the right to face an accuser and the applicability of the Fifth Amendment (rights of the accused). Although it didn't deal with the First Amendment (press freedom), which some board members expressed an interest in, the board found this memorandum especially relevant when it was introduced.

Then there was the matter of supporting witnesses. I had selected some friends I felt would be positive additions at the hearing and called all of them in advance. First on the list was Irv Stone, *Aviation Week* Los Angeles Bureau chief and my immediate boss until his recent retirement. Bruce Peterson, NASA experimental test pilot and marine reservist, agreed to testify. Col. Lou Bass, longtime Marine Corps friend and past commander of my marine A-4 squadron at Los Alamitos and Maj. George Cannon, operations officer at the Marine Air Reserve Training Detachment at Los Alamitos also agreed to speak on my behalf. All would be impressive and gave valuable testimony.

10

The administrative discharge board hearing

The basis for the hearing was the commandant's two-page, single-spaced letter, signed by L. V. Chapman, Jr., which began:

"During October 1966, this headquarters received information indicating that a series of articles authored by you, and appearing in various issues of the Aviation Week & Space Technology *(AW&ST), revealed detailed information concerning United States' tactics and equipment in use in Vietnam, the disclosures of which were highly detrimental to combat operations and significantly beneficial to the enemy.*

"The receipt of this information resulted in your transfer from VMA-241, Marine Air Reserve Detachment, Naval Air Station Los Alamitos, California, to an inactive, Class III reserve status, pending the completion of investigations in your case (reference MARTC Spl. Order 10-67 of 30 Jan 1967). Following the completion of the investigation, the matter was referred to the Department of Justice with a view toward considering your prosecution for a violation, or violations of Title 18 US Code, Section 793(d) for divulging classified information. The Department of Justice elected to take no action in your case, and all matters were returned to this Headquarters for disposition."

The letter's paragraph 2 follows:

"A summary of the investigation conducted in your case is appended as enclosure (1). Based on its contents, it is considered that, at the very least, you used extremely poor judgment in divulging information which has been described as being significant operational and tactical disclosures to the enemy. In this connection, it is noted that you violated reference (b) which states, in part, that no person in the naval establishment shall convey or disclose by oral or written communications, publication, or other means, except as may be required by his official duties, any information whatever concerning the naval or other military establishment or forces, or any person, thing, plan or measure pertaining thereto, when such information might be of possible assistance to a foreign power."

With the letter and attachment as the evidence for the board to consider, the hearing itself started August 4, 1969, and ended August 8, 1969. The board consisted of three Marine Corps Reserve colonels placed on active duty: Col. Frank L. Eddens, Col. William A. Dougherty and Col. Collin H. Rushfeldt. Eddens and Dougherty were both aviators.

The board was actually conducted by Brig. Gen. Henry Williams Hise, commanding general of Marine Corps Air Station, El Toro, in Santa Ana, California. Brig. Gen. Hise had assigned the responsibility of overseeing the hearing to his judge advocate general (JAG), Lt. Col. Daniel McConnell. He, in turn, had assigned one of his lawyers, Capt. C. Ward Beaudry, USMCR, as recorder, giving him responsibility for running the proceedings. Board members and the defendant were in the uniform of the day.

A verbatim record was made by a court recorder which totaled 411 pages of double-spaced testimony. Several years later, the McGraw-Hill copy was forwarded to me in a kindly gesture since I couldn't afford the $1,000 price tag at the time. The following is based on that court record.

At the outset, there was some confusion over how the board should proceed.

Col. Dougherty: "Would you tell us what this is all about? How about an opening statement?"

Capt. Beaudry: "On March 11th, 1969, Major Plattner received a letter which has been presented to you as Exhibit 1, mailed by the commandant to Major Plattner offering him an opportunity to resign his commission in the Reserves. The letter states certain facts, and is based upon these facts that this board is convened. Major Plattner requested the board, in accordance to SEC NAV Instruction 1900.2, dated 24 May 1955, and this is the board which has been convened today."

Col. Dougherty: "Fine, we know we are a board, but would you tell us the facts? What do you expect to prove?"

Capt. Beaudry: "Sir, I am not going to prove anything. The commandant has submitted a letter to the board for them to consider, and Major Plattner has requested this board hearing, and based on the statement from the commandant, you will be required to make certain findings and recommendations in accordance with SEC NAV Instruction 1900.2."

Col. Eddens: "It is my understanding that this SEC NAV Instruction requires the nature of the circumstances."

Capt. Beaudry: "Yes, sir."

Col. Eddens: "And you intend to present to us the nature of the acts of omissions charged against him?"

Capt. Beaudry: "Sir, as an enclosure to the letter from the commandant, you will see there is a summary of the case of Major

Plattner. It is this summary that the commandant has sent to you that you are to consider."

Col. Dougherty: "Do I understand that's all you plan to do? Do you have other documents you are going to introduce or show us?"

Capt. Beaudry: "No, sir."

Beaudry went on to explain his role in the hearing: "May I say at this time, Colonel, that this board was convened for the purpose of consideration of the letter from the commandant and that summary, and my job here is not as an adversary, but as a recorder to this board to assist the board, and whatever I can do to assist the board I will do, of course. Further, I will also attempt to advise the board, although the board certainly doesn't need any advising in view of their experience. Might I say, sir, that it would be my recommendation to stay within the summary from the commandant of the Marine Corps."

With the board's mission established, it was only to consider the commandant's letter and, primarily, the summary enclosure. The board then retired to read the document after copies were supplied for each member. A full reproduction of the SUMMARY has been included in Appendix 2 for the sake of reference.

Once they reconvened, O'Rourke began by attacking the letter and its summary from a legal standpoint, suggesting that the entire pretrial investigation of the matter be supplied to the respondent. O'Rourke listed numerous legal petitions resulting from previous hearings for the board to consider as a basis for the request. Included were legal renderings that dealt with such things as the accused's right to face his accuser, the right to cross-examine to confront hearsay evidence and the First Amendment (freedom of the press).

Capt. Beaudry: "In the first place, there was a request for a pretrial investigation. I know of no trial, and I know of no pretrial investigation, counsel of the respondent has stated 'pretrial investigation.' I can only state, of course, that this is not a trial. This is an administrative hearing, and I know of no pretrial investigation."

Col. Eddens: "Just a moment. In this report, he is talking about the pretrial investigation conducted by the Department of Justice."

O'Rourke: "The Department of Justice and the Naval Investigative Service and also DINS, I think it is Directorate for Inspection Services at the Assistant Secretary of Defense level."

Beaudry was unfazed by the request to make available the extensive investigative material accumulated in the case, including the efforts to prosecute the case in a civil court under the Espionage Act. Beaudry was unyielding, and he continued to focus the board's attention only on the commandant's letter and its summary. As far as producing the one witness identified by name in the summary, Lieutenant Commander Johnson of the *Kitty Hawk,* Beaudry said there was no basis for presenting him at the hearing, but interrogations in writing would be allowed (this direction did not have much appeal to the defense since the hearing already was underway and Johnson's whereabouts were unknown).

By this time, Colonel Eddens had assumed the role of board overseer as kind of a judge in charge, and he suggested that the hearing be terminated for the first day and resumed on day two at one p.m. to allow members to study O'Rourke's petitions and other matters.

When the board reconvened on day two, O'Rourke's six legal petitions designed to call attention to the respondent's legal rights were discussed in some detail by Colonel Eddens. All six were overruled, which meant that the hearing would go on without spending more time on them.

Nevertheless, O'Rourke lived up to my expectations of being a competent defender against the innuendo-filled and frequently inaccurate letter and the summary attachment. At this point, O'Rourke was not ready to throw in the towel on the discovery and got permission from the board to ask Beaudry some questions to try to learn of the motives behind the commandant's letter. He bored in on Beaudry to get some information about his trip to Washington, D.C., to review the files in the case.

> **O'Rourke:** "Well, let me ask you what documents did you investigate in Washington?"

> **Capt. Beaudry:** "Oh, I saw a myriad of documents. I saw documents that were approximately four, five inches thick that were classified from secret to top secret, and they are not before the board, and they are not for the board's consideration. And the commandant has sent a summary for the board to consider, and it is the government's position in this case that the board is confined in their consideration to the summary, and that the summary adequately informs the respondent of allegations of the commandant, and the board, in fact, gives him an opportunity to present his side and his rebuttal and his explanation, if one exists, to the summary."

> **O'Rourke:** "How long did you spend reviewing this file of documents?"

> **Capt. Beaudry:** "Approximately five or six hours."

> **Col. Dougherty:** "Did you receive any instructions from anyone in the Department of Defense . . . or anyone in any branch of the armed services, as to how to handle this case?"

> **Capt. Beaudry:** "No, sir. I received no such instructions."

O'Rourke continued in a questioning mode, pursuing legal technicalities, such as the MACV guidelines attached to the SUMMARY. He claimed they only related to those who briefed the press, not the reporters, themselves. Other issues were discussed, such as the commandant's statement in his letter that Major Plattner "at the very least, used extremely poor judgment in divulging information which has been described as being significant operational and tactical disclosures to the enemy."

On the commandant's derogatory accusation, the board took the position to examine the evidence. It went on record that it would decide whether to accept the claim and not just approve it at face value because it came from a higher authority.

This set the tone for the hearing and provided a solid hint that the board did not plan to function as a rubber stamp and would make its own decisions on the evidence received.

O'Rourke's somewhat lengthy discovery questioning also allowed him to skillfully introduce the board to much of the correspondence from congressional inquiries as well as the letters I had written, none of which had been provided by the Marine Corps. These letters and documents painted a much broader and clearer picture of the case than the extremely negative and inaccurate letter and SUMMARY attachment.

I had prepared a master file of all relevant information in advance, and O'Rourke cleverly drew on this file to make sure the board received copies establishing a complete picture of what had taken place in previous years. This was despite Beaudry's initial direction to the board to make their decisions based only on the letter and its attachment.

At this point, it was apparent that the board wanted to get into the meat of the rebuttal testimony and leave discovery behind. This brought to a close day two of testimony.

Day three opened promptly at 9:00 a.m. with testimony from the first of four witnesses that I had selected, Bruce Peterson, a National Aeronautics and Space Administration (NASA) research engineer and test pilot. Bruce also was a flyer in the Marine Reserve. I knew him both as a weekend warrior and on a professional level as an *Aviation Week* reporter since I had responsibility for covering activities at the National Aeronautics and Space Administration (NASA) Flight Research Center at Edward AFB, California, where he worked.

Peterson described two research programs with which he was personally familiar and on which I had written stories for *Aviation Week*. The first was a paraglider recovery system for the Gemini space capsule, and the second was flight testing of the HL-10 lifting body vehicle on which Peterson was the test pilot. Peterson was testing the unpowered HL-10 prototype when several unforeseen problems cropped up at the last minute, and he crash-landed the vehicle on a dry lakebed. He suffered some injuries (the video of the crash was subsequently used as part of the introduction to a TV series called *The Six Million Dollar Man*).

> **O'Rourke:** "And lifting body programs . . . Could you describe the nature of those programs?"
>
> **Peterson:** "The lifting body program is a flight investigation of re-entry vehicles for the recovery of vehicles from space programs which I think would be the next generation of space vehicles. We are doing flight research on those things."
>
> **O'Rourke:** "Have you ever heard any discussion which would cast doubt on the reputation for truth and veracity of Major Plattner?"
>
> **Peterson:** "No, I haven't."
>
> **O'Rourke:** "Now, in regards to his reporting activities, did he appear to use discretion in reporting on the matters with which you were personally familiar?"

Peterson: "Yes, I believe one particular case in point was the first flight of the HL-10, which I made in December of 1966. He was afforded the opportunity to attend our technical debriefing on the flight during which everything was discussed openly. And I don't know of any other reporter that's ever been allowed to do this. We hang out our dirty laundry or anything else that may come up, and I believe that Tony could have used some of the information to question some of our engineering capabilities or judgment, and he did not."

O'Rourke: "Have you or any of the persons to whom you directly report ever requested that he not publish some facts?"

Peterson: "Yes, I guess on one occasion on the lifting body, there were stability and performance numbers which were classified, and in the normal course of things, Tony was allowed to know the lift and drag ratios that we had reached at certain speeds, and we asked him not to report those because they were at that time classified. These have since then been declassified, but at the time they were classified, and he did not report them."

O'Rourke: "Did he follow your request not to publish that information?"

Peterson: "That's correct. On another occasion, he did report the accident of the MTFT (HL-10) which I was involved in, although most of the report was actual tapes and the official accident report of our board, and it was accurately published in *Aviation Week*."

The board members realized that they were hearing from a uniquely qualified test pilot and a very knowledgeable marine reservist and continued to pepper Peterson with questions relating to items in the SUMMARY until the lunch break. This covered the waterfront with queries on the following topics: how classified was the

A-4, the design of the A6-A Intruder, the subject of Pathfinder aircraft, the SA-2 missile and how it worked, the Pop-Up maneuver and when it was practiced in the Marine Reserves on an unclassified basis, the Douglas F-3D and its equipment, the Republic F-105 and its bomb bay, loss rates for the F-105 and A-4, the TPQ-10 radar used by the Marine Corps, the Marine Corps use of fixed-wing aircraft for helicopter escort, the McDonnel F-4C Phantom design and, minimum pullout altitude for dropping a 250-lb bomb.

Peterson did not have complete answers to all the questions, but he fielded each with honesty and insight. His responses were all unclassified and provided board members with a general understanding of the depth of unclassified information prevailing at the time.

The board also asked Peterson if he had discussed the Marine Corps with Major Plattner, asking if he cherished his position as a marine officer pilot. The answer was "Yes, sir." Also, in response to the question of "Have you ever heard anything derogatory about him from Marine officers?" he replied, "No, sir, I have not."

The hearing resumed at 2:00 p.m. with testimony from Maj. George W. Cannon, USMCR (Ret), who had been operations officer at the Marine Air Reserve Training Detachment (MARTD) at NAS, Los Alamitos, when I was still actively flying in the reserves. The MARTD consisted of two A-4 squadrons as well as a support squadron that contained a TPQ-10 radar. By the time of the hearing, Cannon had retired from the Marine Corps and was flying as a civilian first officer for AirCal.

O'Rourke: "Can you tell us in your own words what access to classified data Major Plattner had during the year 1965?"

Cannon: "His access was the same as all the other Reserves, normally only confidential material and that only in direct connection with their job. Specifically, the only thing that he ever had access to was the sight settings, bombing information for the A-4 as necessary to perform the mission in the A-4. Also fuel planning data that we used, and the fuel planning data was for the training which was an airplane with two drop tanks and a practice bomb rack normally. There was no other need for any of the reservists to go any deeper in classified material at that time."

O'Rourke: "And did the Marine Reserve Training Detachment control any classified data that was available for Reserves?"

Cannon: "Yes, we had classified material, but as far as for the Reserve's use, it was principally because it was required for the Detachment's use."

O'Rourke: "Now, were you acquainted with a demonstration of the so-called pop-up maneuver that was made in Southern California during the year 1963?"

Cannon: "It was at the Marine Corps Base, Twenty-Nine Palms. The people that I was acquainted with there, of course, were mostly the marines in Operation Desert Wind. There were a number of newspaper reporters in attendance for some of the demonstrations that came after the maneuvers were over. I was there as a liaison officer from MAWTU PAC (Marine Air Weapons Training Unit Pacific) at that time commanded by Colonel Michelson."

O'Rourke: "Now, was there anything classified about that demonstration?"

Cannon: "Not to my knowledge because it was a demonstration for the people in attendance there."

O'Rourke: "When Major Plattner returned from Vietnam, were you interrogated by any agents of the Naval Investigating Service concerning his reporting in Vietnam?"

Cannon: "Yes, I was."

O'Rourke: "Can you tell us the substance of his inquiry to the best of your now recollection?"

Cannon: "He asked me if I had read the articles and if I had found anything in those articles that would be of a classified nature. I told him I had read the articles, and I didn't see anything that was classified. He asked me then if the total concept of the articles, even though any one of them was not classified, if, in my opinion, the total concept of all of them together would make them classified. I told him that this was out of my jurisdiction, and really I didn't know. As far as I was concerned, if they weren't labeled classified, they were not classified."

O'Rourke: "With reference to that conversation, did he also query you considering Major Plattner's access to classified information prior to his trip to Vietnam?"

Cannon: "Yes, and he got the same answer that there is nothing other than the basic information necessary to fly the A-4 airplane."

O'Rourke: "Now with reference to your knowledge of Major Plattner's reputation, both in the aviation industry and as a Reserve officer, to your knowledge, is he trustworthy and loyal?"

Cannon: "I would say very trustworthy, and I definitely consider him loyal. In fact, I feel that it was his sense of loyalty that caused him to go there to write these articles and that, if anything, that sense of loyalty is probably his main trouble he has with this right now. There were, in my opinion, of course, many predictions and comments upon the way we conducted the war that are not really provable, but they were opinion and hearsay from others in the area which mirrored the opinion of many of the people I met that have been to Vietnam. But the Department of Defense, in particular, may have taken some umbrage at that. They wouldn't be politically happy to hear the fact that if we didn't change, we would drag the war on forever, and it's still going."

As with Bruce Peterson, board members had numerous questions for Cannon because of his particularly relevant and extensive knowledge of the Marine Reserve operations at Los Alamitos and marine aviation in general.

Included in the questioning were the following topics:

- Protection of classified material: "In regard to that question of classified material, all people who handle classified material are warned that if they have knowledge of certain classified material and they see it later in print, say in a newspaper or magazine or in any other form, they can't confirm the veracity of this information because that would really break the classification. Therefore, when I read the articles with my knowledge of what our classified material contained, I saw nothing that I would have to corroborate as being true, because it wasn't touched on in a classified manner."
- Level of clearance held by Cannon: "Top Secret" (as a member of the high security MAWTU PAC; also one level above the normal secret clearance held by pilots).
- On the question of a movie showing the F-105 dropping bombs, Cannon replied that he had not seen it.
- The Shrike antiradiation missile: "It's a rocket that homes in on certain enemy radar frequencies, and the pilot gets a signal in the cockpit when it's locked on, and he punches the button and the rocket flies to the target and hits it. In essence, that's the idea of the SHRIKE."
- The reputation of Shrike in 1965: "Mostly it had come near the target but had only destroyed it a couple of times. I heard people say that it hadn't arrived up to the expectations."

- SA-2 SAMs: "I have heard some comments that as far as they could tell, it was the greatest thing that ever happened. When the enemy launched a SAM, it was a complete waste of money, and they were pretty spooky looking as they went by, but they hardly ever hit anything."
- Pathfinder aircraft: "A Pathfinder is generally an aircraft specially equipped for a certain type of target. As in the present war, they are generally used because of their electronic equipment to find enemy radar sites and either avoid them or attack them as the mission dictates. The other aircraft in radio communication follow along behind and either make the attack or attempt to avoid the radar-controlled guns or missiles or whatever their mission happens to be."
- Types of Pathfinder aircraft: "The A-4s and A-6s are the only two I know of."
- Rating of Plattner as a pilot: "I thought he was an excellent pilot. He was very proficient in all of the items we trained in, bombing, rockets."
- Rating of Plattner's service and background: "Major Plattner was one of the few people that would always make that extra effort in the Reserves. I was particularly impressed in 1966 because he was given a job of writing up the historical report for the maneuvers for his squadron. Of all of the units I had that gave me this report, his was the best and most lucid and clear. Of course, his experience as a writer would bear that out, but it was done on time and with a great deal of hard work and effort going into it. He was also one that was always there for every drill and made the additional night training periods; very dependable person. We don't have any parties. His reputation isn't from being out there as a good-time man, but as a worker."
- Additional details on the Twenty-Nine Palms demonstration

per a question from Beaudry: "Colonel Michelson was leading the flight of A-4s that made the pop-up maneuver and
so, as they were coming in on the pop-up, the announcer
described their approach, and they came at a very high rate
of speed for the type of pop-up which would be used, primarily against a missile site, with their leader coming up straight
ahead and making a very fast half roll, putting the nose to the
target, and then they dropped practice bombs in the practice
area and the wingmen rolled off to the right and left. They all
hit the target right on the nose. Then the helicopter escort . .
. There were three A-4s escorting a helicopter into an area,
and you could see them doing a series of pull-ups and dives
as the helicopter approached. There in the stands, they had all
the reporters and all of the off-duty personnel that could be
spared to watch the demonstration."

After a short recess, O'Rourke introduced Col. Lewis N. Bass,
the third character witness. Col. Bass was commanding officer of the
29th Staff Group at Los Alamitos and had known me since 1953 when
serving together in VMC-2 at MCAS Cherry Point, North Carolina.

O'Rourke: "If we were to ask you the same question we asked
Major Cannon about Major Plattner's reputation in the squadron
and specific acts that he performed, would your testimony be the
same?"

Col. Bass: "I think it would be the same and possibly a little stronger because I feel that I knew Major Plattner probably a little
closer personally than Major Cannon did, and if I had to make
a fitness report out on him today, it would probably parallel the
ones I made out on him which showed excellent performance,
excellent pilot, a good Section D write-up, and I would particularly desire to have him."

Col. Dougherty: "Can you ever imagine Major Plattner doing anything intentionally that would hurt the United States?"

Col. Bass: "In my opinion, he very definitely would not."

The board asked a few more questions about Col. Bass's combat experience, to which he replied that he had flown forty-five to fifty combat missions in World War II and 100 in Korea. He held a current rating at Los Alamitos in the A-4. The board then thanked him for his testimony and went to direct examination of Major Plattner.

At this point, the board was anxious to hear from the respondent and get on with rebuttal. O'Rourke spent the remainder of the day leading me in testimony by tracing relevant background information from high school, college, then into the navy flying program and ultimately becoming a marine aviator. It included work history in the family newspaper business, followed by a transition to *Aviation Week* as a journalist.

An especially important segment dealt with my trip to Vietnam as a reporter employed by McGraw-Hill, the parent of the magazine. The testimony went into great detail about how I had been selected by *Aviation Week*'s editor, Robert Hotz, to travel to Vietnam for two months to gather information and report on the air war there. Pan Am commercial transportation was used routing through Guam, where I visited Anderson AFB to interview crews of B-52 bombers stationed there.

Before leaving, I checked out of my reserve squadron for a two-month leave of absence. Also, I took my reserve ID card out of my wallet and left it at home since I was not traveling as a marine reservist and did not want to be mistakenly identified as such.

When I arrived in Saigon, I secured temporary quarters and then moved to a permanent room at the Mondial Hotel because of their short supply. I maintained the room for the whole period I was there.

It was paid for with my McGraw-Hill expense account, which also was used to cover all other expenses on the trip.

After returning home, I wrote my stories mainly at the office of my employer, McGraw-Hill, in downtown Los Angeles and at home. As a weekend warrior, I resumed flying in my reserve squadron VMA-241 under orders from my Marine Corps employer for the time spent in training at NAS, Los Alamitos, as a reserve pilot on monthly drill weekends.

The testimony clearly linked my reporting solely to my civilian job, which was completely unrelated to the military. The commandant's letter, however, tried to establish a rationale for their case against me by stating that I had violated a navy regulation in my reporting. Paragraph 2 of the letter states:

"Based on the SUMMARY'S contents, it is considered that, at the very least, you used extremely poor judgment in divulging information which has been described as being significant operational and tactical disclosures to the enemy. In this connection, it is noted that you violated reference (b) Art 1252 US Navy Regs 1948, which states, in part, that no person in the naval establishment shall convey or disclose by oral or written communications, publication, or other means, except as may be required by his official duties, any information whatever concerning the naval or other military establishment of forces, or any person, thing, plan or measure pertaining thereto when such information might be of possible assistance to a foreign power."

In addition to this nonexistent violation of Article 1252, the SUMMARY declared in paragraph 5: "The following excerpts, relating to aircraft tactics, losses and combat maneuvers in apparent violation of the COMUSMACV policy letters, were contained in PLATTNER's articles of 24 January, 7 February, 14 February and 21 February 1966 issues of *Aviation Week & Space Technology Magazine*" (followed by five single-spaced pages of MACV guideline violations).

A copy of the guidelines attached to the SUMMARY which every in-country reporter was asked on a volunteer basis to observe, is summarized:

- A suggested set of voluntary guidelines titled RELEASE OF COMBAT INFORMATION, primarily for operations in South Vietnam, requests reporters to withhold details of progress in ongoing military operations to keep such timely tactical information from falling into the hands of the Viet Cong or North Vietnamese. In general, however, these guidelines allow reporters to write about what they see and hear when in the field or when flying as an observer in an aircraft.
- A set of ground rules titled RELEASE OF AIR STRIKE INFORMATION establishes what military personnel can say to reporters on combat activities. There are twelve such rules that provide a framework for releasing air strike information as soon as it is available. Included are targets and locations, types of aircraft and whether land or water-based, number of crew members picked up, time of attack, success of the mission, ordnance expended, number of strike aircraft, types of aircraft involved, weather en route and over the target, enemy antiaircraft fire and sightings of unfriendly aircraft. In addition are eight restrictions which should be observed for security. Included in this category are takeoff information, including site and time, damage reports, tactical specifics on altitude, course, speed (may use terms such as "low" and "fast"), future strike information, weather problems, rules of engagement and enemy reaction.

Reporters must acknowledge receiving the guidelines by their signature. I did sign the guidelines as part of the check-in procedures, and I took them seriously. The strange accusation that there was extensive information being protected as classified and that these MACV guidelines were violated by the disclosure of classified information in my stories was purely an invention by the summary's authors to provide a prosecutable case. The use of the MACV guidelines as a foundation for security violations illustrates how a case can be developed from scratch without any factual basis and boldly built into a serious-sounding but phony accusation with no real evidence to support it. Nothing in my stories violated the reporter guidelines, and I reported what I heard from speaking with personnel in the country in the presence of information officers. I tried very carefully to abide by the guidelines. I could not have, in any way, violated security regulations because I had absolutely no access, at any time, to the protected classified documents that were cited, which made the charges even more ridiculous.

The meaning of the reporting guidelines was explored further:

O'Rourke: "Did you later discuss the nature of those policy letters with army Lieutenant Colonel Biandi who was at the MACV Public Information Office?"

Plattner: "He tried to help me understand it."

O'Rourke: "What was the substance of what he told you?"

Plattner: "Essentially, Biandi's interpretation to me of the meaning of it, as far as I was concerned, was that when he found out the type of reporting that I was doing which was gathering information in Vietnam, planning on writing the stories after I got back to the United States, and he found out that I worked for *Aviation Week* which writes about aviation things, so his interpretation to me was essentially that it didn't have much application to me. There was one thrust in particular that the air strike policy letter was trying to get across, and that was one of timeliness. They didn't want reporters going out into the field and reporting things immediately to their newspapers, wire services, or TV networks which would help the enemy in the midst of a troop engagement or air operation—the type of thing where the enemy would be reading about it in the newspaper with the operation going on at the same time and might be able to receive a combat advantage from it."

O'Rourke: "Now, nobody at MACV or at the Special Projects Office claimed to be attempting to censor reporters' conduct, did they?"

Plattner: "No."

The questioning by O'Rourke continued and covered my two face-to-face encounters with the Naval Investigative Service, the suspension of my secret clearance, followed by removal from flying status.

This allowed O'Rourke to put on the record a number of letters from my master file that were sent and received, such as my mast request with the commandant.

The investigative arm of the navy's Office of Naval Intelligence (ONI) is the Naval Investigative Service (NIS). These agents gather information and write reports on the subject under investigation. These reports are never made public and therefore are never subject to examination to verify their accuracy, so usually, there is no opportunity to refute the information they have gathered unless, in the case of Lieutenant Commander Johnson, testimony was unclassified for the purpose of prosecution.

The SUMMARY document attached to the commandant's letter undoubtedly was filled with NIS investigative reports. Some of their conclusions were misleading, and others were untruthful for whatever reasons—speculation without verification, shoddy reporting or the like. An interesting recollection of a meeting with NIS agents at the *Aviation Week* office in February 1963 establishes the defendant's side of the confrontation over the A-2F story I wrote shortly after joining the magazine. One can only guess what the agent put in his report.

O'Rourke: "What was the substance of Mr. Arrigo's conversation with you at this meeting?"

Plattner: "Mr. Arrigo wanted to know who I had spoken with at Grumman Aircraft Engineering Corporation, where I had gone to get information for the A-2F story. He wanted to know the names of people I had spoken to, what they told me, and he kept repeating this theme over and over again. He would find different ways to couch the inquiry, but it was always the same thing, kind of like a broken record. He was always coming back to the same point again, who did you talk to, almost a badgering technique."

O'Rourke: "Now, what was your impression of Mr. Arrigo's attitude at the end of your conversation?"

Plattner: "Well, I thought he wasn't too bright in the way he went about it. He knew certainly from the outset that I wouldn't tell him who my sources were. We got that out of the way right at the beginning, and yet, he kept on pursuing it, and he had gone about it different ways trying to sneak in the back door, as it were. I did go to great lengths to try to convince him that I had had no access at Grumman because I had had none. He would say, 'Well, did you walk by a room where perhaps there was this open classified secret document on a desk or was there some writing on a blackboard that you may have seen as you walked by?' Of course, I said no. And he'd mention, 'Well, who did you check in with when you went in, and after you checked in, who did you talk with?' He kept on going at it over and over again, so I finally wrote a statement. I said, 'Okay, I'll write this statement.' And

I said, 'I have had no access to classified information while at Grumman,' and I signed it and gave it to him."

O'Rourke: "Did he appear to you to be angry at any time during this conversation?"

Plattner: "Yes, he and Mr. Stone had an altercation. It was toward the end of the interview, and Mr. Stone advised him that the line of questioning seemed unreasonable. Mr. Arrigo seemed to become incensed by Mr. Stone's saying this."

(Later, in discussing this NIS visit with a friend in the regular Marine Corps who had had a lot of experience with NIS agents, he, first off, did not hold the caliber of the agents in high regard, and he ventured that they probably gave me an uncooperative rating in their report.)

Late in the afternoon and nearing a wrap-up for the day, O'Rourke asked about how I gathered the information for my stories.

O'Rourke: "Did you subsequently then, after receiving accreditation, travel around Vietnam in your reporting activities?"

Plattner: "I did."

O'Rourke: "And there was no effort on the part of MACV to censor any of your activities in collecting information, was there?"

Plattner: "No, there was not. There was no effort to censor activities as far as gathering information other than the normal filter channels that you run into when dealing with sources. If this is classified, you don't talk about it, but no attempt to censor."

O'Rourke: "Now, insofar as your travels are concerned in Vietnam, did you contact information officers from all the services?"

Plattner: "Yes."

O'Rourke: "Where did you go in the beginning?"

Plattner: "Well, the first place I went was Tan Son Nuit air base, which is right outside of Saigon, for information on the B-52s."

O'Rourke then asked if I had contacted information officers in the Army, Marine Corps, Air Force and Navy and had acquired all my information in unclassified interviews with the knowledge of information officers. (If you are out in the field in an operational situation or if riding in an airplane, information officers typically were not present). The answer was generally, "Yes, there were information officers present." When the conversation turned to detail the trip to the carrier *Kitty Hawk*, Colonel Eddens suggested that this was a good place to end the third day's testimony.

Day four of the hearing started with detailing my visit to the carrier *Kitty Hawk*. Extensive preparation had been done to rebut this part of the charges since the only individual mentioned by name in the entire SUMMARY was Lieutenant Commander Johnson, a maintenance officer in an A-6A squadron. As detailed in the SUMMARY, his testimony claimed that I had violated a promise to have my manuscripts approved and that I had shown him a Marine Reserve ID card. Both accusations were incorrect.

O'Rourke: "Now, McBride, Ensign McBride, is he the information officer then for the A-6 Group?"

Plattner: "He was the information officer for the *Kitty Hawk*."

O'Rourke: "In talking with McBride, did he introduce you to the people aboard the *Kitty Hawk* in the A-6 Group?"

Plattner: "Yes."

O'Rourke: "Can you recall some of the people you talked with?"

Plattner: "I talked with Lieutenant Commander Johnson, for one."

O'Rourke: "In reference to Commander Johnson, did you show Commander Johnson a reserve identification card?"

Plattner: "No."

O'Rourke: "Did you tell Commander Johnson that MACV ultimately would censor your notes?"

Plattner: "Absolutely not."

O'Rourke: "Did you tell Commander Johnson that MACV had given you permission to quote percentages?"

Plattner: "Commander Johnson and I had a discussion about percentages since he was the maintenance officer of the A-6A squadron, and the A-6A had been in a lot of trouble from the development standpoint for years. I asked him how the availability was at the present time. The squadron was the second A-6 squadron to deploy. The first had deployed previously that summer, and Johnson indicated that the A-6 was coming along pretty well. I said, 'Well, what kind of availability are you getting, and is there some way to show the fact that the A-6 is doing pretty well compared to its previous poor reputation?' We discussed some availability figures in reference to a time when the A-6s were virtually grounded or at a stand-still previously. And since I had, in talking with other people throughout Vietnam, asked the same question about the availability of aircraft, and information officers had been in attendance, the interpretation had always been made that it was permissible to talk about percentages of availability as long as you didn't get into aircraft totals—the one thing that MACV was very set on was expressing a total number of aircraft in a squadron and then attaching a percentage to it as if you had twelve aircraft in an A-6 squadron, and you gave that figure. Then you said they averaged about 50 percent availability. Well, you know you have got six airplanes flying all the time. This is the type of thing that MACV tried to get away from. I explained this to Johnson. He gave me the figures on availability the previous fall compared to what they had at the present time, and he was still a little queasy about it, so I suggested that I get an opinion from the CO, and he said, 'Fine, go ahead. If they say go ahead, use it.' So I took the figures that he had given me, and I went up and talked to the CO and the XO. I said that Commander Johnson suggested that we go over these things, particularly the availability figures. We discussed the information a short time, and they said, 'Yeah, go ahead. That's fine.' Incidentally, I might add that throughout my writing, I did adhere to this general restriction on providing totals of aircraft on a unit basis, and in writing about the *Kitty Hawk*'s complement, for example, I gave no individual squadron's totals. I only gave an approximate total number of aircraft on board the ship, although I did know, of course, the individual totals."

O'Rourke: "Do you recall whether you indicated to Commander Johnson that you were also a pilot?"

Plattner: "I may have. I can't recollect."

O'Rourke: "Do you recall whether you indicated to Commander Johnson that you had been in the Marine Corps Reserve?"

Plattner: "I would have to give the same answer because if I had indicated it, or as sometimes happened, an information officer who had found out I had been a pilot would introduce me as 'Here's Plattner from *Aviation Week*. He's a pilot.' Normally, when I talked to people, I gave no indication that I was a pilot. If it were discovered in the course of the conversation like somebody would say, 'Gee, you know quite a bit about airplanes. Have you ever been a pilot?' I would say, yes. Then he would ask, 'Where did you fly?' and, of course, we would naturally talk, but I never used it as an introduction into any interview, the fact that I was a pilot and a marine reservist."

O'Rourke: "Did you talk to other officers?"

Plattner: "I would estimate twenty-five to thirty, including some civilians (tech reps) who were on board."

Col. Eddens: "In the SUMMARY, Lieutenant Commander Johnson declined to discuss electronic countermeasures or armament. Did you ask him any questions about electronic countermeasures?"

Plattner: "I don't recall either asking Johnson a straightforward question about whether he had ECM equipment or any details about ECM. MY primary purpose in interviewing him was to discuss maintainability, and I hadn't intended to discuss armament, what they carried or that type of thing. I wanted to talk about whether the airplane was up or down, and if it was down, why, and if it was performing good and why. I didn't get into these aspects with him. I did ask other officers those questions."

Col. Dougherty: "Just so there will be no mistake about this, in the SUMMARY, Johnson alleged that he tried to hold the conversation to routine matters; however, Plattner wished to discuss maintenance aspects of the A-6 aircraft. Is this true?"

Plattner: "That's true."

Col. Eddens: "I noticed that Lieutenant Commander Johnson believed that Plattner had shown him a reserve identification card."

Plattner: "No, sir."

Col. Eddens: "Did you have your red card with you on the trip?"

Plattner: "I left it home."

Col. Eddens: "So you couldn't have shown him the reserve identification card?"

Plattner: "I chose not to take it with me."

Col. Eddens: "But you did show him your MACV correspondent's card?"

Plattner: "I believe I did." (The MACV card was marked as exhibit I.)

Col. Dougherty: "Isn't it probably true that you never really had an interview with a pilot that it didn't come out somewhere along that you were a pilot or had been a pilot?"

Plattner: "No, that's not quite true. As a matter of fact, when I went down to the Marine air base at Chu Lai, the A-4 outfit there, I talked to the operations officer late into the night and gave no indication that I was a pilot at all. I didn't tell him until I left the next day because I didn't want him thinking that I was a buddy-buddy A-4 pilot I and it would be permissible to give me information."

Col. Rushfelt: "You were requested to appear in the office of Mr. Arrigo, and you declined. I'd like to have you give your explanation of why you so declined."

Plattner: "When Arrigo and Chenowith located me in the Lockheed parking lot, we talked for perhaps twenty minutes, and we made a tentative agreement to get together at his office. This was on a Saturday at about 6:00 p.m. It was tentatively set up that we would get together Monday afternoon. At that time, I was interested in why they were interested in me. I had gone through the previous inquisition with them, and I suspected what they wanted, but I wanted to gain a better understanding of it. The other fellow mentioned a navy story and a marine story I had done because I had queried them. Of course, you don't get much out of ONI people, but he did mention those two stories. In the morning, I, of course, called my editor, Mr. Hotz. We discussed it, and he indicated that it would be very foolish, and I concurred immediately, to go down to his office, certainly without a witness. The reasoning for not going to his office, I presumed, was that his office would be somehow electronically bugged. I would be alone and would have no one to witness whatever statements I made. And at any rate, they wanted to talk to me about something I had done as an *Aviation Week* reporter. It seemed that the burden should necessarily shift to them. They should come to my office if they wanted to talk to me, and I made this clear. I expressed a willingness to cooperate and said I'd be glad to talk to you on anything that I can talk about, but you'll have to come up to the office in the presence of a witness for me."

Col. Rushfelt: "The second question I'd like to get into is the fact that you and your immediate superior refused to divulge any names of anyone who had given you information at the aircraft plant you visited. Is that a common procedure with your magazine?"

Plattner: "Yes, it certainly was. It was a very strong policy of the magazine and me. It's a tradition, of course, in journalism not to disclose sources."

Col. Eddens: "That's a standard practice among journalists not to divulge sources?"

Plattner: "It's always been a standard practice."

Col. Dougherty: "You gentlemen have a code of ethics under which you operate, right?"

Plattner: "Yes, we do."

Col. Dougherty: "Take the phrase 'off the record.' If you came and talked to me, and I wanted my remarks off the record, you would either say I'm sorry and not listen to me, or else, if you did listen, you would never be able to write what I said, right?"

Plattner: "There are differences in interpretation of that phrase 'off the record,' and the differences lie in the individuals who use it. Your interpretation may be that it should not be written about whatsoever. Others may interpret it to mean that it's all right to use the information as your background in your writing but don't quote me as saying it. So I always try to get this clarified at the outset when I'm talking to somebody. Often, when I talk to them, they will want to carry on the conversation on a nonattributable basis. That means that I cannot attribute it to them as an individual, and then you need to clarify whether I can attribute it to perhaps the firm or an official of the firm or whether we have to get even broader yet and say maybe an industry official. So you must clarify your ground rules, and I spend quite a bit of time clarifying ground rules as I did in Vietnam."

Col. Dougherty: "Isn't there a statute in the State of California that says a newspaper man does not have to divulge his sources?"

Plattner: "I don't know that specific statute, but it's my impression that this has always been upheld constitutionally, not just in California."

At this point, Beaudry was allowed to ask some questions on my background for what he deemed was compliance with the SEC NAV

INST 1900.2 to elaborate on my civilian and military history more fully. The SEC NAV Instruction was the governing document for the administrative discharge board underway. Beaudry's detailed questions were not adversarial and simply dealt with where I was born, where I grew up, schools attended, sports participation, work history, including joining *Aviation Week,* entering the military and where I served.

Following this somewhat lengthy discourse, the last of the four favorable witnesses, Irving Stone, was introduced. Mr. Stone was a twenty-three-year veteran at *Aviation Week* and was the Los Angeles bureau chief when I joined the magazine and throughout my Vietnam reporting. He had recently retired from McGraw-Hill, and as a consultant, he held the position of West Coast editor for the Air Force Association's publications.

> **O'Rourke:** "Did you attend an interview sometime in 1963 between Mr. Plattner and yourself and a Mr. Arrigo from the Office of Naval Intelligence?"
>
> **Stone:** "I was there. Yes."
>
> **O'Rourke:** "I would like to show you from a summary this paragraph 11 which purports to describe that interview. It is part of a several-page summary attached to the government's evidence in this case."
>
> **Stone:** "It is substantially correct except where it says that during the course of the interview, I interrupted on several occasions advising Plattner not to name his sources for the articles nor furnish a formal statement concerning the matter. I did advise him not to furnish a formal statement. The reason for my interruptions was that after Mr. Plattner refused to divulge his sources, the investigator kept coming back to the same question, asking Mr. Plattner to reveal his sources. Frankly, I said this was becoming monotonous

and was wasting time. He came back to the sources perhaps five or six times during an hour of interview."

O'Rourke: "Did the investigator leave you with any impressions insofar as his attitude was concerned?"

Stone: "Well, he was unhappy. He was not pleased with the interview and the fact that Mr. Plattner would not reveal his sources."

O'Rourke: "With reference to revealing sources, does *Aviation Week* have a policy in that regard?"

Stone: "I would unhesitatingly say that it is a policy of the magazine not to reveal sources. The interview is generally considered to be of a confidential and personal nature, and as such, it is a private relationship between the two."

O'Rourke: "And is it your understanding of the nature of confidential communications between a reporter and an interviewee that the First Amendment of the Federal Constitution gives you the right to keep those communications confidential?"

Stone: "That's my interpretation of it."

O'Rourke: "Now, insofar as your knowledge of his reputation in the aerospace industry, could you tell us what kind of reputation he has?"

Stone: "I would unqualifiedly state that his reputation in the aerospace community is excellent. He is considered reliable, trustworthy and honorable. I've never heard anyone, and I repeat, anyone, say anything derogatory as a result of any relationships that Mr. Plattner has had with them as a reporter or otherwise."

O'Rourke: "Does that include the military complex and the journalism community?"

Stone: "Yes, it would."

O'Rourke: "As bureau chief in the Los Angeles office during the years 1965 and 1966, did you receive any comment or criticism of Major Plattner's Vietnam articles from any agency of the federal government of the United States?"

Stone: "None at all."

O'Rourke: "Do you know of any criticism or comment by any agency of the federal government of the United States directed at *Aviation Week* as a result of Major Plattner's Vietnam articles?"

Stone: "Not to my knowledge."

Col. Dougherty: "How does *Aviation Week* determine whether something is classified or not?"

Stone: "My policy was that if you thought that the information might be classified, you inquired as to whether it was, or whether it might be, and if it were, you didn't want to know it."

Col. Dougherty: "Could you tell us the procedure by which these articles were edited and printed?"

Stone: "It was a rather difficult assignment because when Mr. Plattner returned, the schedule set up was that one of these articles was to be published each week. This put rather a substantial burden on Mr. Plattner. The articles were written frequently at home to avoid distractions and telephone calls at the office. And the bulk of them—I think there were thirteen or fourteen articles—were teletyped, usually the day before or the day of the deadline, which generally was a Wednesday. They were teletyped to Washington. They were not edited by me."

Col. Dougherty: "Who would have edited them?"

Stone: "I wouldn't know who edited them there. I would presume that they came to the attention of Mr. Brownlow, although that is only a presumption on my part."

Col. Rushfelt: "Articles are written by staff writers such as Major Plattner and are transmitted directly to your head office for printing without coming to your attention or anyone in your office. Is that correct?"

Stone: "This was not always the case. With a new man, you generally checked his stuff for accuracy of presentation. This was in keeping with the procedure used for any new man who comes aboard. I never considered it necessary in Mr. Plattner's case, and with these particular articles, to the best of my recollection, the schedule was so tight that they normally were transmitted almost directly at the deadline."

O'Rourke: "Could you give us your impression of Major Plattner's capability as a reporter?"

Stone: "Well, I would recommend him most highly. Frankly, I know of no one in my twenty-three years with McGraw-Hill and about twenty years with *Aviation Week* whom I would consider a more competent reporter and a more diligent and industrious reporter."

O'Rourke: "Certainly, he was a reporter who would not give any information in a story which might possibly aid some enemy?"

Stone: "I don't think Mr. Plattner is oriented that way at all."

The board then thanked Mr. Stone for his testimony and broke for lunch. Afterward, Captain Beaudry requested an opportunity to pose some questions. Although his questions were sometimes quite specific and bordered on cross-examination, they generally did not have an adversarial tone, so Col. Eddens allowed him to continue. However, O'Rourke watched him like a hawk, and on several occasions, objected.

Capt. Beaudry: "Now, if we can go back to your meeting with Mr. Arrigo and your prior testimony in 1966 when he met you in the parking lot, and then he talked to you over the telephone a couple of times following that meeting. Is it your contention that this agent of the NIS, Arrigo, was persecuting you?"

O'Rourke: "I object to the question on the grounds that it's not only argumentative, but it's inappropriate from the point of view that he is here simply to develop facts."

Col. Eddens: "I think it should be rephrased."

Capt. Beaudry: "When did you last see or hear from Mr. Arrigo?"

Plattner: "I heard from him during the final conversation over the telephone in that October general confrontation."

Capt. Beaudry: "Now, you did state in your testimony that what you took to be veiled threats were given to you over the telephone, is that correct?"

Plattner: "Yes."

Captain Beaudry: "You stated that he told you that he wanted you to come down to his office for many reasons, one of which was because he had a direct telephone line to Washington where service officer qualification jackets were available, and I think you gave a couple of other reasons that you said he stated. Is that correct?"

Plattner: "That's substantially what I remember I said."

Captain Beaudry: "What exactly were these threats?"

Plattner: "When I told him that I could not and would not go to his office and that he must come to my office, one of his responses at that point was, 'I am going to have to make a call to San Diego and tell somebody about this.' One of the items I mentioned previously was his statement that there are 'some very high-level officials who are going to be very interested in your reply,' indicating that if I did not cooperate with him by going to his office alone, there was an ominous quality to it. There was something sinister about it, something like a big old summer thunderstorm brewing up out there heading this way."

Capt. Beaudry: "You have stated that in 1963, you went to Twenty-Nine Palms for a demonstration. How did you come to go there on that particular occasion?"

Plattner: "The office received an invitation from the Marine Corps, and Irving Stone thought it would be a good idea if I went up there. It was a press junket in connection with a SATS (Short Airfield for Tactical Support) showing. They also had a fire power demonstration at the same time. They picked the press up in a DC-3 at Burbank Airport, and I was one of a number of reporters from the Los Angeles area who got on the airplane and flew there and back after the show. I didn't write an article. It turned out to be more of a background-type than anything else."

Capt. Beaudry: "Do you remember what was said during the demonstration concerning the type of target that would be involved in the 'pop-up' maneuver you viewed?"

Plattner: "I know that surface-to-air missiles, or SAMs, were mentioned, and this was the type of maneuver you would use against a target defended by SAMs. I remember that the maneuver itself, 'pop-up' was specifically mentioned."

Col. Eddens: "Did you read an article, I believe in the *Los Angeles Times,* that explained that it was a technique for a low approach to escape radar surveillance so he could get up to a target without being discovered and pop-up?"

Plattner: "I believe that the *Los Angeles Times* and/or the *Herald Examiner* did write such an article."

Capt. Beaudry: "You have spoken to the board concerning two army articles you wrote. And in talking about this, you indicated that you did not print all the information you gathered intentionally. The information that you did exclude from the articles that you eventually wrote, what was the reason for excluding this information?"

Plattner: "One of the stories I wrote was about the armed Mohawks flown by the army at Vung Tao air base. An air force information officer got me aside one day and said, 'Do you know the army is flying armed support for troops?' So I did look into it and asked the army permission to do a story on armed Mohawks, which was quite a sensitive subject. However, I was given permission."

Col. Eddens: "Was it sensitive to the army because they were, in effect, doing close air support for their own troops, and it was supposed to be an air force job?"

Plattner: "Yes, it was a roles-and-missions argument. The army information officer called up the commanding officer of the Mohawk outfit at Vung Tau and made arrangements for me to go down there, and unlike the air force, he provided no transportation. He told me a place where I could stand and maybe hitch a ride on a helicopter, which I did. I arrived at Vung Tau and wandered around and found the commanding officer of the group. I told him I was there to do a story on his outfit. At the time, the army was flying OV-1As, a photographic version of the Grumman Mohawk. They also were flying OV-1Bs and OV-1Cs. The OV-1B carried a side-looking airborne radar known as SLAR. The OV-1C carried an infrared device known under the general code name of 'Red Haze.' The SLAR and the Red Haze were very sensitive surveillance equipment.

"I rode on a mission in an OV-1A over the delta. In fact, it was two missions interrupted by one refueling, which lasted for about four hours, on which I reported altitudes and speeds, this type of thing because it was allowable. When we got back from the mission, I wanted to report as much as they thought was publishable on the OV-1B and OV-1C, so we adjourned to the officers' club. We sat around over a few beers and decided, or they decided, what was unclassified information, and what was common knowledge on the SLAR and Red Haze versions. During these conversations, considerably more information than I ultimately used about the capabilities of the OV-1B and OV-1C came out. We decided at that time, based on their decision, that some of these things they had mentioned should not be used, and I did not use them in my articles."

Capt. Beaudry: "You decided not to use some of these things because you thought they were classified or because you just thought they might have been classified?"

Plattner: "That's a hard question to answer. I don't think anybody there, certainly, myself included, could say whether those things really were classified or not. The criteria we used were common sense, good judgment, what it seemed would be able to help the enemy, what he'd like to know. Nobody went to a document to find out if something was classified or not."

Capt. Beaudry: "Did you make your determination while in

Vietnam concerning what you would include that they thought was all right to print?"

Plattner: "We made the determination on the spot. They made the determination with my concurrence. I relied on their judgment, and I added my judgment when I thought it was pertinent. I was in no position to know whether anything was classified or unclassified."

Capt. Beaudry: "We are on the *Kitty Hawk* now, and you testified that you don't remember asking Lieutenant Commander Johnson about electronic countermeasures. Was the primary purpose of speaking with him to get information on the maintenance aspect?"

Plattner: "My purpose in interviewing Johnson was for the maintenance aspect of the A-6A."

Capt. Beaudry: "You stated previously that you did ask others about electronic countermeasures and armament."

Plattner: "I asked the question of two or three other officers if the A-6 had any electronic countermeasures gear, and I was told it didn't, and that was the end of the conversation right there. As to armament, I asked what type of armament they normally carry. At that time, they had MERs and TERs on their airplanes. The A-6 originally came out with MBRs (multiple bomb racks), which had been replaced with the MER (multiple ejector rack) and the TER (triple ejector rack), which forcibly ejected the bombs away from the airplane, whereas the MBR just released the bombs and didn't kick them away forcibly."

Captain Beaudry: "Could you have, with your understanding of armament, been able to tell what the different types of bomb racks and the different type of armament that these planes were carrying?"

Plattner: "The date I went to the *Kitty Hawk* was November 28th. I had been in the country for over a month at that time. Prior to my going to Vietnam, if you are trying to allude to the fact that I was an expert in ordnance because of my Marine Reserve flying, it's not true. I knew little about live ordnance before I went to Vietnam. I had only dropped a couple of 250-pound bombs in the Reserve and fired a couple of live rockets. I became a semi-expert on ordnance that was being used in Vietnam while I was out in the zone. I learned to recognize MK-80, MK-81, MK-82, MK-84 bombs and the 250-pound fragmentation bomb and all of the equipment by going out and walking around, asking pilots what they were. I rode along on eight combat missions while I was out there. Most of them had been flown by the time I got to the *Kitty Hawk*. So I became well versed in ordnance from my observations in Vietnam."

After a short recess for the board to caucus on a couple of issues, questioning resumed by O'Rourke on the second meeting with the NIS agents in October 1966.

O'Rourke: "Major Plattner, would you define for us your understanding of the term 'literary license'?"

Plattner: "Literary license, to my way of thinking, is the license the reporter has to describe things the way he sees them."

O'Rourke: "Did you use that term in talking to Mr. Arrigo in October of 1966?"

Plattner: "I did not. The way it's used here appears to refer to the fact that literary license meant I would not divulge my sources of information. The term 'literary license' has no such meaning."

O'Rourke: "Did you at any time during your reporting in

Vietnam lead a military officer to believe that you would submit your notes for a security review by any higher echelon prior to publication?"

Plattner: "Absolutely not. It is a very strong policy of the magazine that we don't submit our articles, or our notes, for clearance to anyone, military, civilian or whoever they may be. And our stories are gained on that basis. Some periodicals, trade journals and the like have a practice of doing this. We do not. I followed our policy in Vietnam."

O'Rourke: "Mr. Hotz, who is the editor of *Aviation Week,* receives telephone calls or other inquiries from the Defense Department, doesn't he?"

Plattner: "I don't know much about Mr. Hotz's business because I've never been in the Washington Bureau. I presume he receives calls from the Defense Department and other people."

O'Rourke: "Let's talk about your case now. Do you know that he received no calls from the Defense Department or any military services critical of your articles on the Vietnam War?"

Plattner: "This is what Mr. Hotz indicated to me by letter." (The letter from *Aviation Week*'s editor in chief, Robert Hotz, to Tony Plattner, explicitly states that neither the Defense Department nor any of the individual services expressed concern over my Vietnam series of articles or contacted the magazine. It became Exhibit 8 of the proceedings record.)

O'Rourke then led me through direct rebuttals of each of the eight subparagraphs of paragraph 7 of the SUMMARY, which reads: "7. At the time the above-mentioned data was published under PLATTNER'S byline, the following items of information were being protected as classified information within the military services but have since been declassified."

Paragraph 7 was part of the foundational charge leveled against me that I had printed classified information that I was not authorized to. It was a strange paragraph implying that I somehow was aware that the specific items were classified and went ahead and printed the information anyway. For this to have happened, numerous sources I spoke with would have had to break security regulations and provide classified information to a reporter with absolutely no need to know the eight listed subjects. At the same time, I would have had to accept the information as being classified and then gone ahead and printed the information in direct opposition to the rules of my employer and my own firm guidelines on handling classified information—this, of course, never happened, nor did the investigating agents ever find evidence of it.

The subparagraphs are summarized as follows: (a) tactics of US aircraft, (b) performance of the Shrike, (c) performance characteristics and countermeasures to SAMs, (d) use of the F-100 as a Pathfinder, (e) bomb bay configuration of the F-105, (f) loss rates of the F-105 and the A-4, (g) operational readiness rates of the A-6 and (h) electronic intelligence missions being flown by Douglas aircraft.

> **O'Rourke:** "Are there any specific tactics which might be of possible assistance to an enemy or might possibly injure anybody in our establishment?"
>
> **Plattner:** "No."
>
> **O'Rourke:** "With reference to paragraph 7(a), in the gathering of the information excerpted in the summary, did you gather it all in unclassified interviews?"
>
> **Plattner:** "All of the information that went into my articles came

through unclassified interviews. There were no classified interviews held in Vietnam."

O'Rourke: "Did you have access in the United States because of your reserve status to any classified information that you used in your articles included in subparagraph 7(a)?"

Plattner: "No."

O'Rourke: "Did you have access in the United States because of your reserve status to information found in subparagraph 7(b)?"

Plattner: "None."

O'Rourke: "Would your answers on the availability of classified information be the same for subparagraphs (c), (d), (e), (f), (g) and (h)?"

Plattner: "Yes."

O'Rourke: "Can you recall where you were at the time you obtained the information for your SAM article?"

Plattner: "The information for my SAM article was gathered throughout the course of my stay in Vietnam. I might illustrate this. These are my notebooks. When I got back, I spent approximately a week cataloging the information. There are eighty sheets in each notebook. There are six notebooks and a part of another book. There are 160 half-size pages in each notebook, and they are all full on both sides. One of the ways I cataloged my notebooks after I got back was to put little tabs on pages so that I could refer to them when I was writing my articles. The blue tabs here refer to the surface-to-air missile story. As you can see, they run throughout the six notebooks, so the information came from a variety of sources and places."

O'Rourke: "Did you acquire information on the SAMs from the 5:00 o'clock follies in Saigon at any time?"

Plattner: "Yes, I did. One of the best examples of that is the SAM envelope map which I constructed based upon those briefings where they indicated where missile sites had been struck, the locations of them in coordinates. I got a set of maps, which I then brought back with me. These were standard aeronautical charts and are available to anyone. I had plotted some of those locations from those briefing sheets handed out at the 5:00 o'clock follies and made up my own SAM envelope. I sent this drawing back to our artist at *Aviation Week* in New York, and he drew it up. We ran it in two colors to go with my SAM story. An example of a MACV handout was submitted and became exhibit I of the proceedings."

O'Rourke: "Can you give us an estimate of the number of pilots from whom you obtained information on surface-to-air missiles, and how many were flying combat missions?"

Plattner: "I would estimate over fifteen pilots provided information, and about one-third were flying combat with the others doing planning and the like."

O'Rourke: "Did the information officers introduce you to the pilots for the purposes of interviews?"

Plattner: "Yes."

O'Rourke: "Was the F-105 story arranged by an air force information officer?"

Plattner: "Yes, air force information officers did arrange for me to do a story on the F-105."

O'Rourke: "Did you discuss SHRIKE with a high-ranking air force officer and a high-ranking navy officer?"

Plattner: "Yes, I did."

O'Rourke: "Did either of these officers indicate that what they told you was in any way classified?"

Plattner: "They did not."

O'Rourke: "With reference to SHRIKE, had there been prior publications of the ineffectiveness of the missile?"

Plattner: "The fact that SHRIKE was a relatively ineffective missile had been discussed previously in several publications including a December 1965 article in *Aviation Week* and another article in *Missiles and Rockets* magazine in October 1965."

O'Rourke: "There's a reference in one of the articles to operational kill rates. Will you tell the board how you arrived at the kill rate?"

Plattner: "I presume you are referring to the kill ratio of the SA-2 missile. I divided the number of aircraft downed by SAMs by the number of missiles that had been fired. This was requested by Mr. Hotz. One of the sources used was a government official who provided a rounded, unclassified answer. I used an article published in *Aviation Week* on January 10th written by another staff member as another source. *Time* magazine also published a figure and was another source. I compared all three, which were similar, and picked a number of 5 percent and sent it off to Washington."

O'Rourke: "Now, about the hunter-killer attack on SAM-equipped sites, had that been published prior to the time you wrote about it?"

Plattner: "Yes, it had been discussed in unclassified briefings. The hunter-killer is kind of synonymous with Pathfinder. It's just a different way of expressing it."

O'Rourke: "Was that information given to you as unclassified by aviators with the permission of their official information officers?"

Plattner: "Yes."

O'Rourke: "The SAM story contains some information obtained from another staff member of *Aviation Week* after you returned from Vietnam, doesn't it?"

Plattner: "Yes. I was kind of surprised to see it when it came out. It was several paragraphs written by another staff member (concerning a SAM site strike which was inserted in the SAM story during editing. It recalled a Pathfinder A-6 leading a flight of A-4s from the carrier *Independence*)."

O'Rourke: "Would you tell us what a 'fishback' is?"

Plattner: "A fishback is this thing in the parentheses, AW&ST standing for *Aviation Week & Space Technology,* followed by the date and page number. For example, January 10th, page 83. It's a means of calling the reader's attention specifically to a previously published piece of information without covering the same ground. When I was putting together the report on the war up North, which included the F-105, we had a situation where the base from which the 105s flew could not be identified.

"At the time, the US was not admitting that strikes over North Vietnam came from bases in Thailand. The official position of the information officers was that they could not identify those bases. I wanted to do the F-105 story, but the bases in Thailand seemed to pose a formidable problem. *Aviation Week* had published previously that we had bases in Thailand and what the bases were, so I indicated to the information officer that I would fish back to that previous *Aviation Week* article to get him off the hook if he gave me the story, and he did, and I put the fishback in."

This brought to a close day four of the hearing with a plan to reconvene on Friday, August 8 at 8:30 a.m. The final day of the hearing continued with a more robust rebuttal of the charges that I had disclosed classified information in violation of regulations. Since we had no knowledge of what information might have been a part of actual classified documents, the path that we followed was to establish that, first of all, every bit of information gathered for the articles while in Vietnam came from unclassified interviews. For added insurance, it was established that much of the information identified in the SUMMARY as classified had already appeared in the open media *before* my series was printed and thus, had been available already to enemy forces.

It was also pointed out that MACV guidelines authorized some of the SUMMARY information. I had not personally written information in some cases, but it had been written by another staff member and added to my stories in the editing process. This part of the rebuttal was important since after leaving Vietnam and returning to Los Angeles to write my stories, there were no local military contacts to update or confirm information.

All the people you would typically call, such as information officers of the various military services, were located in Washington, D.C., so I had to rely on the Washington Bureau to provide any needed updates to my articles. In the editing process, other staff members made additions that were inserted in a seamless way into my articles.

Our rebuttal approach did not challenge the assertion that the list of items identified as classified actually was located somewhere in a secure document (we, of course, had no access to such files), nor did it dispute the rationale for protecting them as classified information despite the fact that simple logic could have come to the same conclusion.

The testimony tried to accomplish that I had played the game of civilian reporter for *Aviation Week* with integrity, honesty and concern for national security. At the same time, we wanted to establish that I had performed as a competent and fair journalist with my status as a marine reservist, never playing a role in my job as an *Aviation Week* reporter.

> **O'Rourke:** "With reference to your SAM envelope, how did you conclude that jet aircraft were the only type of aircraft that could get into that envelope?"

> **Plattner:** "This was a pretty straightforward conclusion. The strikes that were flown against SAM sites and against heavily defended targets were all flown by jet aircraft like F-105s and A-4s. The MACV handouts listed the types of aircraft that flew these missions. Based on this, it was a pretty simple conclusion that they would use jet aircraft with the highest speed available."

> **O'Rourke:** "Directing your attention to the navy story in the February 7, 1966, issue, where did you obtain the information concerning the loss ratio per sortie on A-4s?"

> **Plattner:** "It was provided by another staff member of *Aviation Week* in the Washington Bureau. There had been prior publication of it in *Aviation Week* on December 27th, page 13. It identifies the loss rate as one aircraft for every 350 sorties."

> **O'Rourke:** "Insofar as the pullout and degree of bombing dive, where did you acquire that information for the February 7 article?"

> **Plattner:** "The minimum pullout altitude of 2,500 to 3,000 ft.

and 30-degree dives were from a personal report of a mission flown in the backseat of an F-4G over South Vietnam. It was a strike against a target located northwest of Saigon, and the ground rules allowing actual observations on missions over South Vietnam applied."

O'Rourke: "With reference to the pop-up again, do you have a copy of the *Fighter Weapons* newsletter from Nellis Air Force Base (Nevada), which concerns that particular maneuver?"

Plattner: "This document is neither classified, nor is it 'For official use only.' The featured article is the F-100 pitch-up tactics. It describes in detail the pop-up maneuver. All of these articles, of course, are sanitized through formal military security review. This article provides some of the background of the pop-up maneuver, indicating that it began in 'William Tell-1962' during a tactical fighter weapons meet held at Nellis Air Force Base in September 1962. The newsletter was marked Exhibit P."

O'Rourke: "With reference to the A-6A being used as a Pathfinder, was this inserted in your January article on SAMs by another staff member?"

Plattner: "That is correct. In addition to this, the actual first reference of using the A-6A as a Pathfinder appeared in an article by another staff member December 27, 1965, page 19."

O'Rourke: "Did you acquire information that there was an ECM capability in use, and did you report that information?"

Plattner: "Yes, I was given this information in the course of on-the-record interviews in the presence of an information officer. I did report that information. The term 'electronic countermeasures' refers to detecting when SAMs are fired and to the jamming of enemy antiaircraft guns."

O'Rourke: "Now, did you acquire a lot of specific information concerning these two concepts that you did not report?"

Plattner: "I knew considerably more about these ECM activities than I chose to report. This included limitations of ECM equipment, speed-limiting factors for various types of ordnance and critical altitudes, speeds and ranges."

O'Rourke: "With reference to your judgment in not reporting some of the unclassified information, can you tell us how you would formulate a judgment?"

Plattner: "My technique in choosing not to print information was an application of a personal Plattner Filter, for want of a better word. It was a commonsense approach based on my knowledge of aviation, my background of reporting and what I thought might be of use to the North Vietnamese. Basically, I tried very hard the entire time I was in Vietnam and when I was writing the articles to ensure that no information which I considered useful to the North Vietnamese would be in my articles. I didn't want these guys to fly over North Vietnam and get shot down because of my articles. I was very concerned about it, and I applied this personal filtering technique in addition to all the other filters that strained the information."

O'Rourke: "Your tendency was then to rely on the military officers who gave you the information as to the sensitivity of the information. Is that correct?"

Plattner: "All my interviews were conducted on an unclassified basis with that basis preceding the interview and explained to the interviewees."

O'Rourke: "In your February 14, 1966, article on the marines, did you get information on helicopter escort and ground control radar from marines with an information officer present?"

Plattner: "The marines were probably the stickiest of all services as far as having information officers always present during reporting. There wasn't anywhere I went that I didn't have a marine information officer with me while interviewing pilots."

O'Rourke: "And that's true of the reconnaissance missions of that story cited on page 5 of the summary. [Repeated here in total: Reconnaissance missions over North Vietnam by Ling-Temco-Vought RF-8As and Douglas EF-10Bs (formerly F-3D Sky Knight) of the VMCJ squadron requiring escort by F-4s. These are the only missions flown over North Vietnam by marine aircraft?]"

Plattner: "Yes. Information officers were there."

O'Rourke: "Let's go on then. Concerning the F-105 bomb bay, how were you given this information?"

Plattner: "The information was given me by F-105 pilots who flew the aircraft in combat in the presence of information officers."

O'Rourke: "Do you know whether *Jane's All the World's Aircraft* contains information on the configuration of the F-105?"

Plattner: "Yes, it does. It contains information that a 390-gallon fuel tank could be used in the weapons bay in place of a nuclear store. It also contains detailed information on the J-75 engine, normal mission load, maximum takeoff weight and other information. The J75-P-19W engine is rated at 26,500-lb thrust at takeoff with water injection (reference the W in the title), according to *Jane's*. A three-page *Jane's* excerpt was then made Exhibit S."

O'Rourke: "About subsonic as opposed to supersonic flight, is that a deduction that could be made about aircraft flying in Vietnam?"

Plattner: "The F-105 is a subsonic cruise aircraft, as are all of our fighters which do not cruise at supersonic speed because they couldn't go very far. When you load fighters down with tanks and ordnance, it creates such a high drag that it cannot obtain supersonic speeds. To reach supersonic speeds, you would have to clean up (drop all stores)."

O'Rourke: "Could you explain the fishback in the F-105 story (in the paragraph beginning 'Between 75 percent and 80 percent of air force strike missions are flown by the F-105'?"

Plattner: "This fishback is to a January 10, 1965, article and references a box with a Washington dateline and a headline titled 'Air Force Flew 49,510 sorties in 1965.' It reports that 'approximately 75 percent of the air force missions over the North were flown by Republic F-105 jet fighters, and the loss rate has averaged .005.' I did not author this box. A copy of the previously published box was entered into the record as exhibit T."

O'Rourke: "In reference to missions in which the gun pod on the F-4C was left off, was this information provided by air force pilots?"

Plattner: "Yes, it's a pretty straightforward problem in range calculation depending on how far you wanted to go and how long you wanted to stay on target. The SU-20 gun pod contains a General Electric N-61 Gatling action 20-millimeter gun. The pod has a drag count approximating a 2,000-pound bomb. I chose rather to express this in a very general language without specifics. I might add that there were MiG aircraft shot down with the gun pod in the war. On one of the F-4 missions I flew along on, a gun pod was used for air-to-ground strafing, and all details of it were freely discussed."

O'Rourke: "With reference to paragraph 6(a), which states that the enemy can now be expected to have confirmed data on kill rates, tell us what your research has turned up."

Plattner: "First of all, the words 'confirmed data' are a bit puzzling. *Aviation Week* does not provide confirmed data to anybody. This is not an official government publication. It is not an official publication of DOD. It is a news magazine. In regard to operational kill rates and the SA-2, it would seem reasonable to presume that the enemy had some knowledge and in much greater detail of how many aircraft he had knocked down with his SA-2s. He has his own firsthand experience of watching his missiles fly up and hit airplanes or miss them. As far as inadequacies of the SA-2 missile, this would certainly be known that he was not hitting airplanes with his missiles. He had already, at the time I was in Vietnam, begun an importation of standard antiaircraft weapons to defend his SAM sites because the SAMs themselves could not defend the sites. The fact that the SAM was a sham, as *Time* magazine expressed it, also was widely published previously."

O'Rourke: "In regard to the means of establishing missile alerts, you specifically withheld data, did you not?"

Plattner: "That is correct. There were black boxes installed in aircraft to determine when a SAM was fired. I knew information about how this worked, and I chose not to use it. An additional point I would like to make is that I used deliberately vague language such as other navy aircraft and electronic countermeasures gear which did not identify the model airplane nor the specific equipment."

O'Rourke: "Insofar as US efforts to hunt and kill SAM-equipped sites, that's one of the things that we talked about from a prior publication standpoint. Is that correct?"

Plattner: "There was ample evidence of this in other publications, and in my research, I chose *Time* magazine and the *New York Times* as representative. Both are worldwide in scope. The idea of hunter-killer Pathfinder techniques is as old as twenty to twenty-five years. It was born in World War II when similar operations were conducted in both the Pacific and in Europe. I gave no information on how the United States was actually conducting these operations. I did not report techniques, specific altitudes, speeds, G-forces, pull up points or evasive maneuvers—no tactical specifics whatsoever."

O'Rourke: "Regarding the follow-on statement in paragraph 6(a), 'This accumulation of performance could enable him to alter his SA-2 firing tactics, and to make changes in SA-2 systems which will increase the kill potential of the weapon and force significantly higher loss rates upon US attack aircraft.' Do you have any research on this?"

Plattner: "The Russians, which were the SA-2 suppliers, and the North Vietnamese already had recognized the inadequacies of the SAMs and were importing Triple-A weapons in tremendous numbers as a countermeasure. As one of the pilots told me, the Triple-A up North in the last couple of months has multiplied like rabbits. As far as the hypothetical charge that higher loss rates would be inflicted on US aircraft because of the information in my stories, it turned out that just the opposite actually took place. On January 23, 1967, approximately one year after my SAM article appeared, Cecil Brownlow wrote in *Aviation Week* that only twenty out of 459 aircraft shot down over Vietnam had been downed by SAMs. This compares with ten aircraft killed by SAMs out of 165 total losses at the time I was in Vietnam. This clearly, once again, establishes the wildly speculative and untrue statements made in the SUMMARY document."

O'Rourke: "Insofar as subparagraph 6(b), which reads: 'SHRIKE Anti-radiation Missile, the enemy can now be expected to have improved knowledge of both US tactics and effectiveness in the use of this new weapon, which is particularly sensitive to compromise. Any changes, either tactical or technical, in the enemy's use of his radars could decrease the weapon's effectiveness. The ultimate effects may be to render an important US weapon ineffective, to permit the enemy a lower attrition of his radars, and provide a correspondingly higher effectiveness of the enemy ground radar anti-aircraft warning and defense system.' Have you formed any conclusions?"

Plattner: "I gave no information on tactics in the use of SHRIKE missile. That part of the statement is absolutely inaccurate. As to the effectiveness of the weapon, it would be definitely reasonable to expect that the enemy was aware that SHRIKE was in use against them (since they had initiated countermeasures). The enemy certainly was in a much better position to know whether his radars were blown up than we were. My statement that SHRIKE had proven relatively ineffective certainly added no information to the enemy's knowledge. As to the weapon being 'particularly sensitive to compromise,' SHRIKE's limitations have been discussed in previous articles in the open press."

O'Rourke: "Relative to the last sentence about rendering an important US weapon ineffective and to permit the enemy a lower attrition of his radars and provide a correspondingly higher effectiveness of the enemy ground radar warning and defense system, can you comment on that?"

Plattner: "This conclusion is purely speculative and is not supported by what actually took place subsequently in the combat zone. A weapon becomes ineffective in the field, based on whether it works, not by a statement in a magazine. To establish the inaccuracy of this speculation, I point out an article by Cecil Brownlow in *Aviation Week* February 6th, 1967, page 22, about one year after my article appeared. It reads as follows: 'The reputation of the navy developed Texas Instrument SHRIKE radar homing air-to-surface missile also has improved over the past year. An early tendency to detonate before impact has been overcome, and pilots generally feel that it is doing an adequate job. You point one's nose toward a SAM site, says one pilot, and it closes down its radar'."

O'Rourke: "Let's go to paragraph 6(c) which says, 'The enemy can now be expected to have a broader and deeper knowledge of the tactics which US attack aircraft are employing. Speeds, altitudes, roll-in points, pullout 'Gs,' release altitudes, communications procedures, and similar briefing details are stated'. Can you comment on that?"

Plattner: "I think it's important to break the war into two parts. The war in South Vietnam was fought in a permissive and relatively safe environment, where there were no enemy aircraft, no surface-to-air missiles and no heavy antiaircraft weapons. The heaviest enemy weapons were 20 millimeter and .50-caliber guns. The North was a very tough environment with surface-to-air missiles, enemy aircraft, extensive antiaircraft weapons, including radar-controlled guns up to 100 millimeters and, of course, radar sites and ground spotters. The ground rules for reporting on missions down South were that reporters could write about what they saw and heard without restriction except for the timeliness aspect if an operation were still underway. Reporters were not allowed to ride on missions over North Vietnam. I rode on eight fixed-wing missions over South Vietnam in F-100, O-1E, F-4B, F-4C, F-4G, A-1E and OV-1 aircraft, as well as helicopter flights into various landing zones. I reported many details of these flights, all of which were authorized by MACV ground rules."

O'Rourke: "Can you comment on the conclusion in subparagraph 6(c) that a military pilot faced with continued flying duties in this hostile environment would not be inclined to divulge similar information because of the resultant, obvious possible improvement of enemy capability?"

Plattner: "This is the third conclusion in these three subparagraphs, which is hypothetical in nature and absolutely wrong. The fact is that my articles were based on information provided to me, a civilian reporter, by military pilots flying in the combat environment of North and South, and they gave me more information than I chose to publish. This conclusion obviously was written in the Navy Annex by someone who had not yet been in combat himself, or he would not have written it that way. It just was not true based on my experience, as I think I have brought out previously."

Following this final rebuttal to the SUMMARY's wild accusations in subparagraph 6, O'Rourke turned his attention to entering into the record various letters written by the commandant in response to congressional inquiries on my status. There were copies of letters to Senators Kuchel of California and Mondale of Minnesota and Representative Langen of Minnesota.

The commandant's letter to Senator Kuchel noted that the transfer to Class III was done on a routine, interim basis. The letter added the following: "There is no disciplinary action pending and therefore no charges with which to confront Major Plattner." The Mondale letter repeated this information but added the following, "Whatever investigation the Justice Department might be conducting was an investigation not of Major Plattner's status as a Reserve Marine, but rather his actions while in a civilian status."

This provided O'Rourke another opportunity to ram home the fact that I had never received classified information as a reporter in-country. He asked, "Did you receive access to classified information in order to fly the missions that you flew in Vietnam?"

I responded as follows: "Absolutely none. There were no classified briefings for reporters, myself included, of course. On the missions I flew, I recall at Bien Hoa air base, the air force had a regular sanitized briefing on escape and evasion prior to my flight in the A-1E. It was completely unclassified. This is the way they treated all reporters."

By this time, the number of respondent's exhibits had grown substantially and had used up the entire alphabet with the final addition of Exhibit Z (Zulu), a letter from the commandant to Representative Langen. These additional documents helped provide the board with the whole picture that it needed to make its decision as opposed to relying solely on the very biased and inaccurate commandant's letter with its attached SUMMARY as had been put on the table at the beginning as the only document for the board to consider.

One ironic twist to the case was put on the table by O'Rourke when he asked about a phone call to the magazine's Washington Bureau by the aide to Commandant Green after the publication of my article on marine aviation on February 14, 1966.

I responded that our Washington Bureau chief, Harry Kolcum, called me and said they just got a call from your commandant's aide shortly after my article appeared. He thought that the article was the greatest and asked for permission to reprint it to make it required reading for all his top generals. General Green was the commandant who preceded General Chapman, the author of the letter before the board.

At this point, Colonel Charles B. Sevier, judge advocate general (JAG) for the Third Marine Aircraft Wing stationed at MCAS, El Toro, was made available at the hearing as a result of our request. Col. Sevier had served at Headquarters of the Marine Corps as staff legal officer for the commandant for a lengthy period of time.

O'Rourke: "Can you tell us where you were stationed in 1966?"

Col. Sevier: "From January '66 to June '66, I was in Vietnam. And about August '66 to the end of '66, I was at Headquarters, Marine Corps."

O'Rourke: "During your time at Headquarters, Marine Corps, what duties did you perform?"

Col. Sevier: "I was the staff legal officer for the commandant of the Marine Corps."

O'Rourke: "How long did you stay in that job?"

Col. Sevier: "Two years."

O'Rourke: "In that capacity, did you have occasion to become aware of matters pertaining to Major Clemens Plattner?"

Col. Sevier: "I was aware of the case while I was back there. I don't know when I became aware of it, perhaps '66 or '67."

O'Rourke: "Could you tell us who initiated the investigation of Major Plattner?"

Col. Sevier: "I'm going to have to take what they say here that initial action in this matter was taken on 25 February 1966. I wasn't in Washington then. I don't know how these things came up. Whether all articles are read by people in the aviation field, I suppose everything is read over in the Navy Public Affairs Office as well as in the Department of Defense. Either one of them could have brought this to someone's attention."

O'Rourke: "Did you prepare any of the correspondence, for instance, that letter to Senator Kuchel?"

Col. Sevier: "No. That letter is G-2 (Intelligence) based. There is a possibility that this case came to my office, and one of my lawyers would release it."

O'Rourke: "Did you, from the review of the file or on the basis of your having been requested to provide an opinion, formulate any belief in whether this investigation was commenced at a level somewhere in the Department of Defense as contrasted to the commandant of the Marine Corps?"

Col. Sevier: "The only thing I would have been in on would have been an opinion. The files were not carried in our office. If someone requested an opinion as to legal action, criminal, disciplinary action which could have been taken against Major Plattner, that would be the only thing that I was in on. The only thing I do know, it was begun in Washington."

O'Rourke: "Insofar as your opinion, you may not be able to answer this question, but isn't it true that you advised that there was no basis for a prosecution insofar as the Marine Corps is concerned?"

Col. Sevier: "That would have been an opinion which I gave my client, and I'll have to refuse to answer."

Both O'Rourke and Col. Eddens thanked Col. Sevier, who did his best within his job's constraints to respond to the questions. At the same time, his testimony showed the frustration of trying to plumb the depths of the case against me by using direct examination to shine a light on those who lurked in the shadows of secrecy. One of the things uncovered in the hearing through testimony from Sevier as well as Beaudry was that the extensive file compiled against me was not being held at Marine Corps headquarters but elsewhere in the Pentagon.

At this point, the hearing was coming close to ending with only a few questions left from Beaudry and O'Rourke. Beaudry's questions dealt with whether the high-level sources I spoke with in Vietnam knew that I was a reservist. I replied that they did not. O'Rourke queried Beaudry as to whether Executive Privilege had been claimed in the files he had reviewed at the Pentagon, and he replied that he did not know.

Then O'Rourke launched into a summation: "I would like to direct the board's attention to the commandant's letter of 11 March 1969 in which he states that 'Based upon the contents of the summary presented here, that at the very least you used extremely poor judgment . . . 'Insofar as that is concerned, it's my feeling that based upon the evidence presented to the board suggesting the very strong reputation for truth and veracity of this witness and based upon the evidence given by others that if the commandant were to review it, he too might be willing to change his view.'"

O'Rourke continued: "I think that the most peculiar aspect of the whole case is that as directed by his civilian employer, this man as a civilian reporter collected data and made a report to his employer for publication on the F-105, the SAM and other topics, but no one in the Defense Department to this date has been critical of *Aviation Week,* the publisher of this information. To me, that's a significant paradox that is beyond my comprehension. In no way, as the evidence shows in this record, did his marine background as a reservist relate to his reporting activities. That's the basis of my argument."

Col. Eddens then said, "This matter will stand submitted. As soon as we can, we will prepare our report for the convening authority."

In reviewing the now-completed hearing and the charges listed in the SUMMARY document, it was clear that the "elsewhere in the Pentagon" location of the Plattner file was either the Defense Department, which initiated the inquiry at the Secretary of Defense for Public Affairs level or the navy. The navy had pursued me in a vendetta-like fashion to convict me first in civil court and then in the discharge board hearing from the time I joined *Aviation Week*.

The navy's fingerprints were all over the SUMMARY document presented as evidenced by the following:

Paragraph 6 reads: "on 21 March 1966, **the Air Warfare Division of the Office of the Chief of Naval Operations (OP-05) summarized the significance of the disclosures as follows: . . .**" *(The fact that the Office of Chief of Naval Operations took responsibility for summarizing the significance of the security disclosures identifies them as the basic architect of this document.)*

Paragraph 6(b) reads: "**SHRIKE Anti-Radiation Missile—The enemy can now be expected to have improved knowledge of both US tactics and US effectiveness in the use of this new weapon.**" *(This navy-developed weapon was in use by both air force and navy at this time. The navy's supersecret approach to discussing SHRIKE was contrasted with the air force's more talkative assessment of the weapon's poor performance at this point in the war. It was reflected in the articles I wrote. Substantial testimony was devoted to a rebuttal of this issue during the hearing.)*

Paragraph 9 reads: "**During questioning on 5 May 1966, Lt. Cdr. Raymond F. Johnson, Jr., USN, stated that Plattner interviewed him in Ready Room #3 aboard the USS *Kitty Hawk*.**" *(Johnson, who was a sailor on a navy ship, was the only witness identified by name in the summary, and the navy used this discussion to try to make a case in the previous paragraph 8, which says that Plattner led at least one military officer whom he was interviewing to believe that he would submit his notes or manuscripts for a security review by* *a higher military echelon prior to publication. This was an effort by the navy to concoct a case that I had violated some nonexistent commitment that was robustly rebutted in the hearing. It is likely that Johnson misremembered the details of our conversation, and the agents jumped on this to build a fictitious case.)*

Paragraph 10 reads: **"On 8 October 1966, agents of Naval Investigative Service contacted Plattner . . ."** *(This occasion was one of the two in-person interviews by navy investigators and was added to the SUMMARY in an apparent attempt to cast a cloak of suspicion over my reporting by implying that I was using my reserve position to gain classified information for my stories.)*

Paragraph 11 reads: **"Plattner came to the attention of Naval Investigative Service in 1963 . . ."** *(Paragraph 11 had nothing to do with my Vietnam series but gratuitously recalled the first in-person investigation in 1963 by the navy on the first major story I did for* Aviation Week *on the navy's A-2F airplane. It highlighted the "brand" stamped on me at the outset of my writing career by the navy, which was apparently based on the mind-set that a Marine Reserve flyer should not serve as a reporter for the world's leading aviation and space magazine. This mind-set, which had absolutely no evidence to back it up and was based purely on suspicion, nevertheless, had gradually been infused over time from the navy into the Marine Corps top brass. This was clear from the commandant's negative cover letter.)*

The decision by the hearing board, which was yet to come, would determine whether the defense that we worked so hard on would prove my innocence in the matter.

11

Press coverage of my case begins

On August 9, the day the hearing ended, Don Smith, who covered Orange County for the *Los Angeles Times,* published a lengthy article based on information leaked to him by the El Toro Marine Corps base. The story included selected details on the commandant's letter that had been the basis for the administrative discharge board favoring the Marine Corps' position. Smith quoted the base information officer, Maj. Robert Booher, and staff Judge Advocate General (JAG) Lt. Col. Daniel McConnell on the rationale for the hearing that Maj. Plattner had published classified information without authorization.

This biased coverage was the first to appear in a major newspaper, and although Smith allowed O'Rourke and me to comment on the story, the comments were buried in the body of the story and did little to set the record straight. The move by the Marine Corps to leak the story to the *LA Times* came as a surprise to both Frank and me since we were unaware of it until we got phone calls from the reporter.

O'Rourke spoke at some length to the reporter, but his rebuttal turned out to be more argumentative than persuasive since it had caught us by surprise, and we did not have an opportunity to strategize on an effective response.

Twelve days after the hearing ended on August 21, I got a phone call from Capt. Mike Campbell, the defense lawyer who had been very helpful during the hearing. He reported on an unofficial basis that the board had completed their findings with quite positive results. The Marine Corps, itself, never released directly to me the board results.

The Marine Corps was now faced with the dilemma of how to handle the board's positive findings. The board proclaimed that I had done nothing wrong, either as a reporter or as a reservist, and recommended that I be retained in the Marine Reserve and not be discharged.

Now that the hearing was in the open press, I called an acquaintance of mine, George Wilson, who had been a reporter for *Aviation Week* but now worked for the *Washington Post* newspaper. He was interested in writing a story on my case, and I had given him background information, including the letter, which was the basis for the discharge board hearing. Up to this point, I had asked him to hold off on publishing anything, but now that the hearing was finished, the *Los Angeles Times* had broken the story without my prompting, and the findings were positive, I agreed to let him go ahead with it.

The story, which was a balanced summary of the case, appeared under the byline of George C. Wilson in ten daily newspapers throughout the country via the *Post*'s news service from September 7th to the 21st.

The story's first three paragraphs read:

"WASHINGTON – The Marine Corps commandant, in a letter inviting the resignation of a reserve pilot for what he wrote as a civilian reporter about Vietnam, contends reservists are forbidden by navy regulation from writing anything about the military establishment which 'might be of possible assistance to a foreign power.'

"This unusual position taken by Gen. Leonard F. Chapman, Jr., the commandant, raises the question of whether reservists working as civilians have a special obligation to what they say about the military.

"The case involves Clemens M. Plattner of Rowland Heights, Calif., a Marine Corps Reserve pilot who wrote about the Vietnam air war while working as a civilian reporter for Aviation Week & Space Technology *magazine."*

The article went on to include quotes from Chapman, Attorney O'Rourke and Editor Bob Hotz. Chapman said Plattner violated navy Regulation 1252, *"which states that no person in the naval establishment shall convey or disclose by oral, or written communication, publication or other means—except as may be required by his official duties—any information whatever concerning the naval or other military establishment or forces, or any person, thing, plan or measure pertaining thereto, when such information might be of possible assistance to a foreign power."*

Asked by the *Washington Post* what precedent there was for applying the regulation cited, Chapman said, *"Through their reserve affiliation, all marines regardless of rank or assignment are expected to be fully aware of the importance of safeguarding classified information, particularly information which may be of significance to the enemy.*

"Maj. Plattner, a veteran of 15 years of commissioned service in the Marine Corps, should have been aware of such safeguards. There is no record of any Marine Corps reservist, serving as a reporter in a civilian capacity, having previously violated security instructions or directives."

The article continued: *"Chapman said there has never been a case like Plattner's [come] before the corps before. Asked if strictly applying the broad regulation about supplying information which 'might' assist a foreign power might handicap reservists trying to call the shots as they saw them as civilians journalists, Chapman replied,*

'Inasmuch as correct regulations and other safeguards are explicit on receiving clearance on articles which may contain classified information, it is inconceivable that such information could be inadvertently divulged.'

"Many marine reservists are employed as journalists and correspondents. To the best knowledge of this headquarters, Maj. Plattner is the first journalist with Marine Corps affiliation to be charged with circumventing security measures. It is pertinent to remember that all American journalists in the Republic of Vietnam operate under security guidelines established by CONUS-MACV, regardless of present or past military affiliations."

O'Rourke claimed that "no realistic evidence had been developed which shows Plattner violated any security in what he wrote for the magazine." He introduced a letter from Hotz which said that "the magazine had never been officially notified by authorities in Vietnam or the Defense Department that security had been broken by the Plattner articles."

Chapman's statement that I had "circumvented security measures" had been rebutted in great detail during the hearing. Still, he continued to be fixated on this theme since the case would have wilted away without it.

Coincidentally, Chapman was in Sacramento, California, for a speech to the Comstock Club on September 11, 1969. This was followed by a press conference on September 12 at the Marine Corps Air Station, El Toro, where he said he would answer questions by the media. I immediately made plans to attend and then briefed a CBS TV news reporter friend, Jim Brown, of my situation and asked him to query the commandant on the issue.

With the TV camera rolling, Brown asked the commandant about the results of the hearing in August, and he replied that he had not seen the board's findings and that the purpose of the board was to allow Plattner to present his side of the case. In response to a follow-up question about the reason for the board, he said that it was to determine whether there was unauthorized disclosure of classified material. He said that he had made no prejudgment in the matter and was waiting to hear from the board.

With recently published *Post* and *LA Times* news stories available as background, the press conference became a newsworthy event, and interviews were requested of both O'Rourke and me, which took place at his office in Santa Ana. The event made the six o'clock and ten o'clock news in Los Angeles, and viewers complimented our performance.

Chapman's position was in line with that of the Naval Service, which had tried its best using the investigative group available to it at the Office of Naval Intelligence to establish a case where I had violated various regulations in authoring the articles about the war. Since the Marine Corps didn't initiate nor did it play a role early in the investigation, Chapman had little recourse but to rely on the so-called evidence the navy had accumulated.

Chapman's rise from an artilleryman background to the top position in the Marine Corps included designation as Chief of Staff of the Marine Corps on Jan. 1, 1964, with the rank of lieutenant general. On July 1, 1967, he became assistant commandant of the Marine Corps, and then on Dec. 4, 1967, he was nominated to become commandant. In January 1968, he was promoted to a four-star General and became the Marine Corps' twenty-fourth commandant. Thus, he had served at Headquarters of the Marine Corps in Washington, D.C., since 1964 at the very highest levels prior to publication of my articles in early 1966 and throughout the investigation that followed. Chapman's close familiarity with my case was verified by the numerous letters he had authored to me.

Following the appearance of the article in the *Los Angeles Times,* Don Smith called and asked for a follow-up interview. I tactfully declined, saying that I wanted to see how the results of the hearing played out.

Not everyone was pleased that I had opened up my case to the public through the news media. Irv Stone, my good friend and recently retired bureau chief, thought it was a questionable move. After Hotz learned about it, both he and Martin were in a sour mood that I had moved ahead with the *Washington Post* without their permission—of course, I knew that they would have immediately vetoed it, so I elected to proceed on my own.

Hotz soon fired off a CYA (cover your ass) memo that I had not kept them informed about everything I was doing—the kind of memo one might expect prior to being fired. And when we met during a Society of Experimental Test Pilots symposium in Beverly Hills, California, later in September 1969, he gruffly ignored me.

However, I continued in my job and, with no additional stories in the public media, things seemed to have calmed down at the magazine. I felt somewhat secure that I wasn't going to be fired, but my crusade to return to reserve duty remained an issue in the background.

Month after month passed with no word from the Marine Corps on the board's findings. Then on Mar. 19, 1970, when Chapman was again on the West Coast for a press conference, Jim Brown of CBS News said he had a question for him about Maj. Plattner, who had a hearing in August 1969, seven months ago and still has received no official word. Chapman responded that he expected to make a decision in the next few weeks.

Brown had pulsed the commandant a month earlier on Feb. 16 when he went up after another press conference and asked Chapman what had happened to the Plattner case. Chapman replied that he didn't seem to remember that particular case as he stared at the ceiling and suggested that Brown call his director of personnel for further details.

Behind the scenes in the US Navy, the "loose lips sink ships" crew now seemed to be standing at the railing of the *Titanic* after the iceberg strike if the board's recommendations held up. According to a reliable source, the ferocity of the attitude toward me remained as solid as ever. He reported this verbatim exchange with the navy crew: "Our job is to get the sonofabitch into courts, and since we couldn't get Plattner on a civil rap, we'll get him on a military rap." Another direct quote: "Plattner is like a bulldog; he never lets go."

12

The board finds me innocent of all charges

Although the Marine Corps never provided me directly a copy of the board's findings, I was supplied one by a board member, a full copy of which is in Appendix 1. The board's report is a masterful summary of the hearing and is meticulously and accurately documented. It takes on every accusation and refutes each one in order. The board members approached the hearing purely based on what had been put before them. This was the commandant's May 11 letter with attached Summary combined with the defense's persuasive testimony and extensive documentation.

The board was not cowed by the serious-sounding language and bogus charges in the commandant's letter and took an independent and open-minded approach to their job. This was in contrast to those in the Marine Corps chain of command who perceived their job as carrying out a mission handed to them, that I already had been found guilty of unauthorized disclosure of classified information.

Paragraph 9 of the findings titled **"Our Conclusions,"** included five subparagraphs, which follow in summary form:

a. "The board concludes that no information of a classified nature was contained in the summary excerpts (Exhibit 1) since prior published articles would indicate the enemy had prior access to the subject alleged disclosures."

b. "The policy letters (attachments 2 and 3 to the SUMMARY) merely requested correspondents to abide by the stated policy on a voluntary basis in the interest of military security. It is noted that attachment 2 (release of air strike information) referred to above applies to the release of information on air strikes in North Vietnam only, whereas attachment 3 (release of combat information) applies to the release of information on South Vietnam. We find no violation by Major Plattner from the policies stated in these two attachments."

c. "No regulation compels a member of the press to submit his material for security review."

d. "There is no evidence that he used Marine Corps Reserve status to gain any information."

e. "That there was neither a violation of regulations nor the exercise of poor judgment."

This was followed by paragraph 10: "In view of the entire record compiled by this board, it is recommended that Maj. Plattner be retained in the Marine Corps Reserve. His loyalty to our country and the Marine Corps has been proved conclusively. His retention in the Marine Corps Reserve will be a valuable asset to the service."

It was signed by Frank Eddens, Colonel, USMCR; Collin Rushfeldt, Colonel, USMCR; and William A. Dougherty, Colonel, USMCR.

The three board members selected at Headquarters, Marine Corps, were, in effect, a jury of my peers since they were marine reservists and brought an excellent understanding of military aviation, the nature of the citizen-soldier and an in-depth knowledge of the Marine Reserve program. Each was a successful businessman in Orange County and had a longtime association with the Marine Reserve program. Two of them were lawyers and aviators.

In retrospect, the presentation put together by Frank and me and the witnesses provided the board with a solid and effective defense. It was also apparent that the board saw right through the commandant's letter and its attachment for the phony document that it was. Also, since they were reservists and not in a direct command relationship to the commandant, they felt free to make conclusions that they believed in without worrying about repercussions due to political considerations. It is important to emphasize that there was absolutely no indication at any time that the board did anything but arrive at a completely fair, unbiased and honest evaluation of the evidence placed before it.

It could be argued that Chapman's selection of board members actually provided a basis for a fair and independent hearing, and that was to his credit. However, he may not have anticipated the final results. But there were too many downsides to his actions to give him a clean bill of health, such as his negative hearing letter, his continuous defense of the charge that I had printed classified information in violation of security regulations and the leak to the press at the end of the hearing. Also, in the days yet to come, there were continuing secret maneuvers to prevent my promotion.

When the board completed their findings August 18, 1969, the results were forwarded to Brig. Gen. Hise who immediately put his JAG to work on constructing a response to the embarrassing conclusions. The JAG went to work immediately on writing a creative rebuttal to the positive findings of the board. One source reported that the first draft of the rebuttal was too long, and he worked furiously to trim it down.

Brig. Gen. Hise was an aviator with a long history of flight experience in marine aviation, stretching from World War II to Vietnam. He had commanded various marine aviation units from squadrons to air wings and had achieved a one-star rank in 1968. For Hise, who was undoubtedly looking for a major general's second star, a deviation from the party line could be a death knell for this promotion.

Lieut. Col. McConnell finally staffed a reply that was to Hise's liking, and the board's findings were transmitted with the first endorsement to CMC on September 5, 1969, under the general's signature.

Paragraph 2 of the endorsement read: "Conclusions 9(a) is unjustified and demonstrates lack of familiarity with the security classification of printed matter. Each subsequent publication compounds the loss of security. One compromise does not excuse another."

The board's paragraph 9(a) reads: *"9. Our conclusions, based upon all the evidence available to the board, are as follows: a. The allegation that the information divulged in the articles was 'significantly beneficial to the enemy' was apparently provided Headquarters, Marine Corps, by DOD(DINS), and the Naval Investigative Service Headquarters. The board concludes that no information of a classified nature was contained in the summary excerpts (Exhibit 1) since prior published articles would indicate the enemy had prior access to the subject alleged disclosures."*

Paragraph 3 of the Hise endorsement reads: "Conclusions b., c., d. and e. fail to recognize that the spirit of Article 1252 navy regulations must continue to impact upon the civil employment of a reservist if the reservist desires to maintain an untainted affiliation with the naval establishment. This is particularly true of a Reserve officer who follows a civilian occupation of writing for a publication articles that analyze and comment upon military flight equipment, systems and tactics. No one can say that constitutional rights of freedom of the press are abridged by such observations because there is no constitutional right to be a Marine Reserve officer." (Nowhere in the defense's testimony before the board was the first amendment, protecting freedom of speech, used as a rationale for defending the articles in *Aviation Week*. This first amendment discussion was plucked out of the air by McConnell and gratuitously added to make a seemingly important but actually meaningless point.)

The board's paragraphs 9(b) discussed the conclusion that Major Plattner was physically in Vietnam only by virtue of his status as an accredited correspondent and that no violation of the MACV reporting policies took place.

The board's paragraph 9(c) reads: "No regulation compels a member of the press to submit his material for security review."

The board's paragraph 9(d) reads in part: "The rule of 'security at the source' puts the onus on those who reveal the information rather than on the recipient. He was willingly and specifically issued all the information in question . . . There is no evidence that he used Marine Corps Reserve status to gain any information."

Hise's endorsement had backpedaled from the charge that I violated navy Regulation 1252 in the commandant's letter to suggest that I should live by the "spirit" of it in my job as a reporter.

The endorsement's final paragraph 4 said, **"Approval of the conclusions of this board is not recommended."**

It is customary for journalists who operate by necessity on the unclassified side of the information ledger that once a subject is presented in an unclassified briefing or is printed in an unclassified publication (assuming it is authentic), it is judged to be a fair game from a news standpoint. Journalists have no way of sorting out whether something is classified or not unless, in special cases, they are given a classified document, such as in the Pentagon Papers case, which is a subject unto itself and not relevant in my case.

Now that the contentious Plattner case was again back in the hands of the commandant of the Marine Corps (CMC), he had to weigh the in-depth and very favorable board recommendations with the superficial and largely irrelevant endorsement made by Brig. Gen. Hise.

On September 11, 1969, the package was circulated to key

staff members of the commandant by the deputy director of the Staff Judge Advocate Division, John L. Ostby. Attention was called to the board's conclusion that no classified information had appeared in my articles.

Chapman's intelligence head, Assistant Chief of Staff G2 Division Col. Stone W. Quillian, took this as a challenge and contributed two documents, the first dated December 11, 1969. It was a three-page dissertation responding to the Ostby memo. A second discussion by him was dated March 24, 1969, and was a background document to go with the Marine Corps Press Plan once the news was leaked to the media.

This press plan was founded on the premise that the determination already was made by higher authority that I had disclosed classified information in an unauthorized manner.

Quillian's December 11 analysis dealt with handling classified information and appeared to try to salvage the original hearing premise that I had printed classified information in violation of MACV and navy regulations. He rehashed many of the original charges laid out by DOD and NIS, embellishing them with his view of the proper way to handle classified matter as if I should have been acting as a marine officer with access to classified information while writing my articles for *Aviation Week*—a truly incomprehensible presumption.

He said, "While on active duty and while on reserve duty, Maj. Plattner must have been continuously exposed to criteria, policy and procedures associated with the protection of classified information. Security education, training and orientation are prescribed in several department directives. It is difficult to conceive that an officer with so many years of service cannot be expected to be familiar with at least the rudiments of such regulations."

Quillian then repeated the navy policy that was clearly refuted in the hearing that: "if official cooperation is requested, as would be necessary for visiting a ship, no official cooperation can be afforded by the navy without consent by the correspondent to an official security review of his manuscript."

Repeating this navy policy in his manifesto illustrates one of the frustrations of this case in which a general policy statement that the navy would like to see followed, but is often ignored, is resurrected as if it actually prevailed in my case. There had been absolutely no preliminary discussions at any time with the navy about making my manuscripts available for review. Had the navy insisted on a manuscript review, I simply would have turned down the invitation to visit the *Kitty Hawk*.

In his rambling dissertation, he attempted to explain how commonsense observations can be protected as classified information, meaning that as long as such an observation is in a classified document, then a discussion of it in the open press would be a violation of security rules. "Whether the tactics mentioned in the articles appear to be common sense to any qualified observer or, by the same token, whether the use of the fastest jet aircraft available is also common sense, is not relevant to the question of whether this information was authorized for release or not. The summary of information states clearly that such information was being protected as classified. Whether the policy was necessary or correct is irrelevant; protection was the policy at the time and should have been adhered to as with any policy of higher authority."

Col. Quillian had spent a long career as a ground officer in the Marine Corps trying to scope out the nature of the enemy and their activities, which is the mission of an intelligence officer. Of necessity, this meant protecting the massive, classified files that he dealt with daily. Classified inputs came from many sources, such as reconnaissance vehicles (satellites and airplanes), debriefings of combatants (air and ground) and various other places. So his position of giving a high priority to protecting classified information undoubtedly came from years of doing just that—guarding the secure information that he was immersed in and had to be locked away in safe storage every day when not in use.

In the end, he followed the DOD/navy lead, like a good marine carrying out a mission, that I had printed classified material in my articles in violation of regulations. He voted with Hise: **"This division concurs with the first endorsement by General Hise that the conclusions of the board not be approved because of the reasons mentioned above."**

Both Col. Quillian and Brig. Gen. Hise seemed to take the position that I should have been acting as a marine officer while writing for *Aviation Week* and paying careful attention to remote navy regulations. They also felt that I somehow should have been able to sort out classified from unclassified material in what I wrote. This obtuse position, of course, overlooked my real-world status as a civilian correspondent while in Vietnam and producing my articles on information provided in-country by those fighting the war in unclassified conversations.

The board had taken a very strong position that I was indeed a civilian while working for the magazine and that I had done nothing wrong as a civilian correspondent or as a marine reservist.

The issue of classified national security information bears some examination at this point. Governing the subject is Presidential Executive Order 13528 of December 29, 2009. Under Part One ORIGINAL CLASSIFICATION, the Classification Levels are:

(1 "Top Secret" shall be applied to information, the unauthorized disclosure of which reasonably could be expected to cause exceptionally grave damage to the national security that the original classification authority is able to identify or describe.

(2) "Secret" shall be applied to information, the unauthorized disclosure of which reasonably could be expected to cause

serious damage to the national security that the original classification authority is able to identify or describe.

(3) "Confidential" shall be applied to information, the unauthorized disclosure of which reasonably could be expected to
cause damage to the national security that the original classification authority is able to identify or describe.

Under Part Four—SAFEGUARDING, a person may have access to
classified information provided that:

(1) a favorable determination of eligibility for access has been
made by an agency head or the agency head's designee
(2) the person has signed an approved nondisclosure agreement
and
(3) the person has a need-to-know the information.

In summary, highly sensitive information such as the Pentagon
Papers gets a classification as Top Secret. However, much of the classified information guarded by the government falls into the Secret
and Confidential category. It is notable that guidance on safeguarding
classified information is quite rigorous and requires that the person
receiving the information be approved for access. He must have a
need to know before receiving access.

An *Aviation Week* reporter such as me, of course, never could
pass the carefully-crafted preapproval and need-to-know require-
ments spelled out in the security regulations and thus, could never
be granted access. At no time did anyone ever give me what was
described as classified information in my job as a reporter, nor did
anyone ever try to coax me into using my security clearance as an
access route to pass on secure information.

Current regulations that have been established for embedding
journalists with units in the field give some additional insight into the

handling of classified information. These lengthy protocols put the responsibility of guarding classified information at the source. This means that it is up to those in the military to guard classified information and not transmit it to the embedded reporters. There are means to handle gray areas and accidental exposure of the reporters to classified information, but the rule of protection at the source prevails. Also, there is no requirement for a manuscript review for any embedded reporter.

The discharge board saw through the bogus claims in the letter and attachments laid out as evidence against me and made clear that guarding classified information must take place at the source. They also pointed out that all the information I gathered was willingly passed on to me by those I met with or observed in my travels.

When censorship was practiced in World War II, reporters' stories were screened by the news organization they worked for in accordance with voluntary guidelines agreed to under the Roosevelt administration. When questions arose, the matter went to an assigned censor who had the final say on what could be printed or broadcast. In Vietnam, the reporter was burdened with the responsibility of abiding with the voluntary guidelines without any upstream approval procedures to worry about.

Now that the commandant had the two negative votes versus the positive board's findings, additional delays took place due to more pondering.

The Marine Corps still had an ace in the hole should they choose to play it. Under regulations governing administrative discharges, the Marine Corps could have overruled the board's findings by claiming that they had not considered certain important information. By electing this option—a rehearing of the case—a more favorable result for the Marine Corps and Navy might result.

This avenue had a minefield for the Marine Corps to deal with. The hazards included ongoing probes by various congressmen, the potential of bringing F. Lee Bailey back and inquiries from the press corps now that they had the bit in their teeth. Additionally, the navy and Marine Corps had fired their best broadside salvo with the case they put on the table and not only had missed the target but basically, were out of ammunition.

Chapman had spent many years in the capital of our country, Washington, D.C., and obviously had a pretty good grasp of the game of politics. Early on, I had discussed my case with a senior retired Marine Corps general, and he was appalled at how badly the Corps was handling my case. He labeled Chapman a politician and said if some of the past marine generals had been handling the case, they would have told the navy and DOD to pound sand.

13

CMC renders its verdict retaining me in the Reserves

The game of politics actually turned out in my favor when finally, on May 11, 1970, some nine months after the hearing and over four years following the publication of my articles on Vietnam, CMC rendered its verdict, accepting the board's recommendation that I be retained in the Marine Corps Reserve and not be discharged.

Simultaneously, in the final decision letter to Brig. Gen. Hise, the commandant disapproved of the board's conclusions for reasons initially spelled out in Hise's endorsement of the board's findings. This highly biased rejection of the board's supporting conclusions offered a political sop to DOD/NIS, Quillian, Hise and, of course, the navy, which had fought so hard to convict me. None of this had any real effect on the fundamental ruling that I be retained in the Marine Reserve. Of course, I was delighted after such a lengthy battle to be vindicated but little did I know that the Marine Corps would not let me get away with a clean victory as I was to learn later.

Since I had been removed from Class II status in the Selected Marine Corps Reserve in February 1967 and transferred to the Class

III individual ready reserve, I was inactive while I was focused on getting some resolution of my case and returning to flying status.

Class III reservists are a fairly large group that are eligible for call-up in a national emergency. They drill in organized units, and although they do not get paid for these drill days, they accumulate points for retirement. They also are eligible to perform active duty for schooling or authorized projects. Points and pay are provided for all active duty. A minimum of fifty points is required for a good year.

While awaiting the hearing decision in April 1970, I woke up to the real world and realized that the opportunity for reaching twenty years of good service I needed for retirement was fast slipping away. I joined an organization at Los Alamitos Naval Air Station for Individual Ready Reservists called VTU (AVN)-16 (voluntary training unit, aviation, 16). The following month in May, I received the positive results of the discharge board hearing in the CMC letter, which seemed to chart my course as an Individual Ready Reservist for at least the near term.

I hadn't given up on my crusade to return to flying status, but there were some substantial boulders in the road ahead. The most formidable was that the Marine Corps, in the letter setting up the discharge board, had said the following: "In this connection, you are further advised that this board will not be empowered to submit recommendation(s) which would relate directly, or indirectly, to your possible redesignation as a Class II Reserve officer. Such action is discretionary with the commandant of the Marine Corps."

This set the policy for the chain of command ladder that would have to be climbed if ever I were to regain my flying status—and there are politics at each rung of this ladder. At the training detachment level, which would be the starting point, a regular (not reserve) marine colonel is typically in charge, and the next rank for him would be a star of brigadier general. So for him to flaunt the system could truncate his career.

My immediate focus, however, was to join a reserve unit and be a productive member. I became the training officer of VTU (AVN)-16 (later becoming MTU (AVN)-10) as a mobilization rather than a volunteer unit. Within the next nine years, I continued my training officer duties under three different commanding officers. I started out with a project of building a single command post exercise (CPX) for the staff of a marine aviation group in 1971, and our unit gained recognition as one of the most active and accomplished MTUs in the 4th Marine Air Wing.

Building on our CPX development, we expanded our training capability to include multiple special projects working with different commands when I moved to Seattle in 1979. I played an instrumental role, along with other members of the unit, and handled the bulk of the design, coordination and briefings for the projects.

Also, and with some grumbling from unit members, I initiated an annual Marine Corps physical fitness weekend where members ran three miles and did push-ups and sit-ups to the standards. Although participation was voluntary for Class III reservists, we had an excellent turnout, and members of the unit appreciated being treated like marines.

14

Leaving *Aviation Week*

With the discharge board's positive results behind me, there was another fork in the road ahead that required attention in 1970. That was whether to remain with *Aviation Week & Space Technology* or move on to another job. I had accomplished some notable things, had advanced my reporting skills significantly and felt comfortable with the journalism job. And remaining with the magazine as a Class III reservist perhaps would no longer offer a red flag to the Defense establishment.

It appeared at the time that I no longer was in danger of being fired by Hotz, although both he and Publisher Martin remained grumpy about my solo run to the finish line in fighting my case. They were particularly irked by my bringing the *Washington Post* into the fray. In pondering all this, I took another facet into account, and that was my pay level. Although I had received some raises rewarding my output, working from a pay entry base of $9,000 a year in 1962 within the framework of McGraw-Hill's measured advancement policy did not appear to offer a good long-term financial reward. Also, a much less capable guy had been hired in the Los Angeles Bureau with a salary higher than mine, which was a burr under my saddle. And then, I recalled my friend Irv Stone who had recently retired and received his first disappointing pension check.

No single factor overpowered my decision, but it seemed like time for a change and to put behind me the stressful period of fighting to set the record straight on my reporting and military activities. So, in the spring of 1970, I called a friend at the Garrett Corp., an aerospace company headquartered in Los Angeles, and asked about a job. Garrett was one of the Signal Companies, which was to later come under the umbrella of Honeywell. I had been asked to speak there about the Vietnam air war after my series ran in *Aviation Week,* so I had established relations with some key people there.

I was hired in the public relations department at the corporate level in April with a nice pay increase. After a couple of years, I moved into market development, working directly for the vice president of corporate sales. I then went into field sales and eventually sales at the division level, retiring after twenty-seven years in Oro Valley, Arizona.

Of course, I told Editor Bob Hotz that I was moving on, and he sent me a nice note thanking me for my contributions to the magazine. Years later, I stopped by his Washington office and filled him in on the aftermath of the hearing and my progress in the Marine Reserve while enjoying some drinks at the press club bar with him. It had been an honor to work for this very capable journalism giant, and I expressed that appreciation to him.

15

The Marine Corps takes steps to ensure no more promotions

Behind the scenes at Marine Corps Headquarters, unbeknownst to me, the Marine Corps had not given up on trying to carry out their assigned mission from higher command to deep-six me. On a business trip to Washington, D.C., in March 1971, I discovered, to my great surprise, that my promotion jacket was salted with substantial negative information that had not been there previously.

The documents included the ominous-sounding commandant's biased letter of May 11, 1970, and its extensive one-sided and erroneous summary. It also included the negative Hise endorsement and the negative Quillian comments. But the board's positive findings were nowhere to be found. All told, there were twenty-five documents, including preliminary requests that Headquarters, Marine Corps had selected to be put into my promotion jacket. Also, there was a warning that I was not to be promoted without clearing it with CMC.

After many years of fighting back—with considerable help—against DOD, the navy and the Marine Corps, it seemed that no single event could come as a surprise anymore, but this action reached a new low. How could the Corps, which started at the bottom of the command chain, in my case, took little or no part in the investigation process, transferred me off flying status as a protective measure, then turn around and sandbag me in this way?

It was obvious that CMC had been frustrated by the board's positive results but didn't want to appoint a new board and hold a public hearing because of the potential downside risk of negative publicity. Lt. Col. McConnell, who wrote the Hise endorsement and was solidly in the anti-Plattner camp, privately called the board's conclusions a "whitewash," according to a friend of mine who spoke with him. It seemed obvious that McConnell never paid attention to the board's thorough examination of the case and careful crafting of their conclusions.

Poisoning my promotion jacket with negative information obviously was aimed at getting me passed over from major to lieutenant colonel three times, which would take three years and mandate my retirement from the reserve several years before getting my twenty good years in

So I began preparing for another phase of fighting back. On Jan. 17, 1972, I wrote the commandant a letter on the findings from the March 1971 review of my jacket and pointed out some obvious things such as the missing board findings and the appearance of only negative information. I also noted that no copy of the board's results had ever been formally sent to me despite several requests. I also spent some time rebutting a few of the wacky charges spelled out in the documents again.

At this point, I planned to take remedial action, and I wanted CMC to be aware that I knew about the sandbagged jacket, but I did not want to make them aware of the steps I would take to remedy my salted files. At this point, I felt like I was in a state of mano a mano (hand-to-hand) combat with Marine Corps Headquarters, which would prevail for the next year. I never received a reply to my letter.

In the process of setting the record straight, timing was of the essence since I already had been passed over for lieutenant colonel once, and the promotion board met again in early 1973. So I started the complicated process of figuring out how to use the navy's Board for Correction of Naval Records to solve the problem. Working on the West Coast presented somewhat of a problem in that the Board for Correction of Naval Records was in Washington, D.C., but I was able to time a business trip there in May 1972 to start the process.

The board is part of the Secretary of the Navy Department, which is senior to the Marine Corps and navy and is available to sailors and marines who believe inaccuracies or injustices are reflected in their records. The individual may appear before the board with or without counsel, and the caseload is relatively heavy, so there often are delays. Once the board accepts your request, an examiner is assigned to process the matter.

A request for a meeting with the board in Washington, D.C., was initiated with a letter on May 12, 1972, suggesting a late May-early June time frame based on a planned business trip. The executive secretary quickly replied that although he would be out of town, an examiner would be available to discuss procedures. I followed this up with a meeting during which I reviewed my case's history and the reason for appearing before the board. Now that the preliminary work was completed, I began to organize my petition to the board.

My official application for correction of military records was dated September 1, 1972, and laid out the case for removing the negative information from my promotion jacket. Reserve Marine Colonel William Dougherty, who had been a board member, agreed to represent me as counsel and his offer was appreciated. However, I actually handled all planning, paper work and coordination myself.

My VTU (AVN)-10 commanding officer, Col. Robert Carr, had

written a letter at his request. It provided a very favorable description of my service in the unit. It noted that I had already been passed over for promotion because of the negative information in my jacket. Also included were the discharge board's findings and a short history of my case.

Not wanting to have my case languish as I had become altogether too familiar with in the past, I asked for another meeting. And on another business trip, I met with the assistant to the board's recorder, Charles Curley, on November 10, 1972. I learned that the official I had met with in May had taken no action to assign my case to an examiner, citing a heavy caseload as the reason. I was informed that my case had turned out to be more complicated than initially believed and that the initial reaction to the biased material in my jacket raised a level of concern that I had done something wrong.

Curley asked many penetrating questions that I was able to provide answers to directly. This cleared up much of the suspicion that had been raised in the jacket material. It seemed apparent that our face-to-face frank discussion with logical, precise answers produced a positive perception that I was not tilting at windmills but had a genuine case of injustice that I was pursuing.

I came away from the meeting with cautious enthusiasm, although Curley made clear that no predictions could be made at this point. I wrote an extensive set of notes recalling the meeting, a habit which I carefully followed to provide an accurate account for later recall. My extensive collection of notes from conversations and observations has provided me with the details that I have used to flesh out this manuscript.

16

The Board for Correction of Naval Records requires the Marine Corps to remove all negative information

Then the waiting game began again, and I was pleasantly surprised when I received a letter from the commandant of the Marine Corps dated January 19, 1973, which said the following:

"1. Pursuant to the provisions of reference (a), all material relating to the proceedings of the administrative board convened by the commanding general, Marine Corps Air Station, El Toro (Santa Ana), California, on or about 4 August 1969, together with related correspondence, has been removed from your selection board jacket and filed in your miscellaneous correspondence and orders jacket."

Reference (a) was a directive from the Bureau for Correction of Naval Records dated 16 Jan 1973.

The selection board met the following month, and I was promoted to lieutenant colonel. However, the board did not forget about me, and in a letter some two and a half years later, on June 25, 1975, the chairman of the Board for Correction of Naval Records wrote to me summarizing a review of my case and rebuked the Marine Corps for its handling of my records. The letter said:

"*1. The Board for Correction of Naval Records recently reviewed allegations of error and injustice in your naval records. The Secretary of the Navy has reviewed the proceedings and approved the decision of the board as follows:*

"*DECISION:*

"*That Petitioner's naval record be corrected, wherever appropriate, as follows:*

"(1) To show that his date of rank in the grade of lieutenant colonel is 1 July 1971;

"*(2) To show that his effective date of promotion to that grade is 1 July 1971, with entitlement to the pay and allowances of a lieutenant colonel from such effective date:*

"*(3) That his position on the lineal list be adjusted accordingly; and*

"*(4) That the report of proceedings together with any other document or correspondence relating thereto and any material that it becomes necessary to remove from his record in order to implement this decision, be returned to this board for filing in a confidential file maintained for such purpose, with no reference thereto being made in Petitioner's official record.*

"*RECOMMENDATION:*

"*That the Department of the Navy pay to Petitioner, or other proper party or parties, all monies lawfully found to be due as a result of the foregoing corrections of the naval record.*

"*2. The commandant of the Marine Corps will take the action necessary to implement the board's decision.*"

This rebuke to the Marine Corps by the Navy Corrections Board was for shifting the negative files in my promotion jacket to another folder (miscellaneous correspondence and orders jacket) rather than disposing of them. It was followed by mandating the corrective action of retrieving the material and shipping it to the Correction Board for safe filing and making the proper adjustments to my date of rank to lieutenant colonel, position on the lineal list and pay adjustments.

The Corrections Board's action marked the final chapter in my twelve-year confrontation with the Defense Department and its navy and Marine Corps services. Ironically, the battle began with the Navy Service and ended with the Navy Department.

17

Continuing My Reserve career

I remained in the Mobilization Training Unit at Los Alamitos and later at MCAS, El Toro, after the marine reserves were transferred there. I continued to expand the MTU training capabilities, which my various commanding officers marked as noteworthy on my fitness reports. It turned out that finally, something worked in my favor, and I joined the 10 percent of those on the promotion list to advance in rank to colonel (O-6).

In 1977, the Marine Corps sent me a letter that I had completed twenty years of satisfactory federal service and was eligible for retirement pay at age sixty. My persistence to this aspect of my reserve career with devotion of countless evenings, weekends and vacation days had finally paid off.

Many Class III reservists call it quits when they reach this point of guaranteed retirement, at least, in part, because the non-pay drill status gnaws away at their psyche when they recall that they were paid regularly as a weekend warrior in the Selected Marine Corps Reserve as a Class II member, or perhaps they feel that the Class III label categorizes them as second-class marines.

However, I continued motoring on as an Individual Ready Reservist partly because I enjoyed the camaraderie, partly because I felt I owed something to the many people that helped me get there, and partly because of the challenge I faced as a marine officer in achieving things in this part of the reserve that hadn't been done before.

About a year after the discharge board hearing, I had made one last push to return to Class II status. I met with the head of the Marine Air Group staff at MCAS, El Toro, and representatives of the training detachment to discuss becoming a member. It turned out that being off of flying status for well over the two-year maximum meant that there was no way that I could return to active flying according to the regulations.

So, even if I could find a detachment commander willing to stand behind me (and the chances of this were virtually zero), my quest to return to flying was no longer realistic. The Defense Department and its naval services, in dragging out the resolution of my case over many years, had inadvertently assured that I no longer would be piloting Marine Reserve aircraft in a Class II billet.

After being transferred by Honeywell to the Seattle sales office in 1979, I joined the local aviation mobilization training unit and continued implementing training activities for Marine Reserve units. In a short time, I became the unit's commanding officer, which became MTU (AVN) WA-41. This time, I switched from command post exercises to nuclear, biological and chemical (NBC) warfare.

We developed a training course for Marine Reserve squadrons using formal instruction and hands-on training with the suits and masks assigned to them. It was the first time that most of the squadrons had unpacked their protective gear and learned how to don the bulky suits and masks to perform their duties in the clumsy garb.

We were still in a cold war with the USSR, and NBC training was being emphasized within the military, so our little MTU unit became a popular group on the training menu of many 4th Marine Aircraft Wing Reserve squadrons. In my last year before retirement in 1984, we were gone as frequently as we could round up a training team to meet with various reserve squadrons in the western part of the US. Every two-day weekend course of instruction on-site was fully reimbursed for travel and pay.

I was offered a paid Class II billet in 1983, which I gracefully declined. I was proud of the training vehicle that I had worked so hard to perfect in my unit. I wanted to continue to participate in what I considered meaningful work for the Reserve Air Wing of the Marine Corps right to the end of my military career.

In 1983, I was notified that I had been awarded the Armed Forces Reserve Medal in addition to the Organized Marine Corps Reserve Medal. This recognition, at least, gave me a single row of three ribbons to wear on my uniform. Since I had never flown in combat, which is a major contributor to the number of ribbons, this small display was the best I could muster for twenty-seven years of active and reserve duty in the military.

After being passed over three times for brigadier general (I had no desire to have a star on my collar, nor did I have the flexibility in my job that would be useful to a reserve general), I was happy to fade away with a sunset parade at the Naval Submarine Base, Bangor, Washington, on Hood Canal June 29, 1984. I received a letter signed by the then current commandant, Gen. P. X. Kelley, thanking me for my contributions to the Marine Corps. It felt good to get a letter from a commandant with a positive message.

After being removed from flying status by the Marine Corps Reserve, I joined a group of Skytypers flying SNJ aircraft in a five plane formation to write messages over Southern California. My airplane was No. 6.

While flying for the Marine Reserves at Naval Air Stations in Minneapolis, MN and Long Beach, CA. I flew a variety of aircraft including the Douglas A-1E, the Grumman F9F-5 and the Douglas A-4B shown here.

After 27 years of active and reserve service, I retired as a Colonel during a sunset parade at the Naval Submarine Base, Bangor, Washington on Hood Canal and awaited my pension which started at age 60.

This marked the end of a lengthy period of trying to right the injustice that had dogged me for so many years. When it was over, I felt that I had refuted the charges against me, cleared my name, scuttled the security risk brand assigned me by the navy, and served with some recognition as an honorable and faithful marine officer. Overcoming my challenges while serving with some distinction left me with a positive feeling when I looked back and it made my truncated flying career in the reserves seem less relevant.

18

My Honeywell Years followed by retirement

Work at Honeywell was challenging but in a slightly different way from my eight years at *Aviation Week*. There, I had been challenged on a brand-new adventure that required dedicated focusing on a steep learning curve to becoming a competent reporter in a short time. Whereas, at Honeywell, I was already familiar with the aerospace landscape and could turn my attention to doing my job of developing and selling products to customers.

After spending nine years at Garrett's corporate headquarters at the Los Angeles airport, I earned an opportunity to join the Seattle sales staff selling products to the company's largest customer, Boeing Commercial Airplane Company. Then, in 1985, I was invited to join the sales staff of a brand-new Honeywell company, AiResearch Electronics Systems Division, in Oro Valley, Arizona.

I eventually took over sales of Honeywell's cabin pressure control systems and the division's research contracts, which meant considerable traveling to countries in Europe and Asia. A cabin pressure control system (CPCS) regulates the altitude inside the cabin from takeoff to landing through a system of valves and electronics. As one of three major CPCS manufacturers worldwide—Liebherr, SEMCA and Honeywell—the competition was always intense but I booked significant business for the company.

Then came retirement in 1997 after 27 years with Honeywell. This phase of my life was almost as busy as when I was working for a living. I always had been very family-oriented and I began with a family houseboat trip on Lake Powell, Arizona in the month of June which was followed the next year with sons and grandsons on a salmon fishing trip to Sekiu, Washington in August. We continued alternating these outings for many years with my wife Helen, Tony, Michael and Jacqueline as well as grandchildren Robert and Nick enjoying the fun. My 19-ft. Crestliner boat, Carpe Diem, proved very useful on Powell as well as fishing in Puget Sound.

With the strong belief that physical exercise is the elixir of life, I began jogging at 45 years of age as an incentive to drop my smoking habit (it worked well). While I was working for Honeywell, I would rise early in the morning wherever my job took me and run my three miles before the day's work began—this included running on the beach in Tel Aviv, Israel, the downtowns of Singapore, Tokyo, Moscow, Genoa, Montreal, Sao Paulo, Madrid and many other cities.

Being an avid skier, every winter included a five-day ski outing in Salt Lake City with slope enthusiast friends from Minnesota up into my late 80s. One of my early ski trips was to Vail, Colorado as a guest of friends, Louie and Geri Farrell who owned a condo there—their home was in White Bear Lake, Minnesota. I served with Louie in Korea and in the Marine Reserve in Minneapolis. He became an airline pilot, retiring from Northwest Air Lines and later published his own memoir.

Louie also was one of the leaders of a group of Minnesota Marine Reservists who banded together and published a collection of personal experiences while flying with the Marine Corps. The book entitled *Marine Wings* was a 379- page collection of stories from World War ll on. I was invited to join the group and I contributed two stories of my experiences to the book as one of its authors.

On the spiritual side, I joined the Catholic Church and then became a Knight of Columbus, advancing to the highest Fourth Degree. I was elected Grand Knight of one of the larger Councils in Tucson and won the Star Council award that year.

I volunteered 13 years at the Southern Arizona Veterans Administration Hospital in Tucson escorting patients and among other things, repairing wheel chairs. I was a founding member and Adjutant of a very active Legion Post in Oro Valley, Arizona. Despite the fact that the Post did not have a bar or restaurant, the energy of its members was devoted to supporting veterans and their families in many ways ranging from homeless vets to Guard and Reserve families. This was recognized with many awards. As the Post Adjutant, I invariably was in the middle of all the activities.

Adding to retirement activities were five trips to Europe and 50,000 miles of RV traveling.

One interesting retirement project arose when I was given an ultralight aircraft built by Tom Whitney, one of the engineers I had worked with in the cabin pressure business. Since he was not a pilot, he made a gift of it to me but wanted to see it take to the air with me as the pilot, so he helped me refurbish it by putting new Tedlar plastic coverings on the flight surfaces and installing a recovery chute designed to bring the whole aircraft to ground in an emergency. Until we refurbished it the Lazair had been stored in a trailer for many years in Whitney's yard.

After completing the refurbishment, I found an ultralight field northwest of Tucson and got certified as an ultralight pilot. The lightweight craft (250 pounds maximum) was a very simple rig powered by two chainsaw engines with three-foot diameter propellers. It had a thirty-six foot wingspan, rudder-vator (a combination of elevator and rudder) and aileron controls but no brakes (taxiing was done by foot-dragging). For instruments, it had a simple metal tube plumbed to an airspeed indicator (takeoff and climb speed was an indicated seventeen mph) and an altimeter measuring feet above the ground. Climb rate was 250 feet per minute.

I flew it often out over the desert, soaring with the hawks and buzzards but always keeping an eye open for emergency landing sites. On its final flight, I was doing a touch-and-go when a crosswind gust from the left started to drift me to the right as I was taking off again. In trying to stabilize the clumsy craft, I got into a pilot-induced oscillation (there was no independent rudder control) and I pushed the tiny throttles forward as far as they would go. The midget motors strained to maintain flying speed, but it was to no avail, and the craft stalled out and fluttered into an acacia bush to the right side of the runway, coming to an abrupt stop, doing some damage to the landing gear and other parts of the plane. Unlike the ultralight I was not damaged but I decided that this would be a good time to call an end to my flying career.

I packed the underpowered and poorly equipped craft into its trailer and donated it to charity. Thus, my piloting days came to an end and, ultimately, I turned my attention to less hazardous activities such as sitting before the computer and putting this memoir together.

19

Looking back and pondering my case

In looking back on the decade-plus years spent fighting to clear my name, it was not until this memoir was completed and all the various pieces of the jigsaw picture were put into place that the massive effort to prosecute me came into clearer focus.

Drilling into the secrecy shroud that blanketed this case was not easy in real time, and only with the help of congressmen and Lee Bailey did the covering come off, one layer at a time, to reveal first one insight and then another. The Marine Corps has always had a close relationship with Congress, given the continuous fighting over roles and missions within the Defense Department. This tended to work in my favor since the Marine Corps always tried to be responsive to members of Congress. At one time, the commandant responded to seven senators and representatives, who were knocking on his door asking about the Plattner case.

One puzzling aspect of the case remained and perhaps will never be crystal clear. Why had the two highly qualified senior officers running the navy and Marine Corps maintained such a negative attitude toward me despite the complete lack of evidence that I had done something wrong? Perhaps the answer was, and this was hinted at by some sources, that they had come to believe I actually had committed criminal acts in my reporting.

Since I had very little visibility on what was happening early on, I, at first, believed that the main thrust behind the effort to prosecute me came from either President Johnson or Defense Secretary McNamara since the pressure seemed so unrelenting. However, during all the investigations performed by the magazine, many friends of mine and the hearing testimony, no real indication surfaced that Johnson or McNamara personally continued to drive the case forward after they had kicked it off. This does not mean that they were not in the background, but they were not visible if they were.

When I was sent to Vietnam to report on the air war there and began publishing the results in early 1966, the navy's efforts, kicked off by McNamara's Defense Department, moved into high gear with beaver-like intensity aimed at building a case for prosecution.

The Marine Corps did not become a major player in the game until well after my stories appeared in the magazine in early 1966. However, a year later, in February 1967, the Marine Corps, sensing the possibility of a national controversy with the prosecution by the Justice Department of one of its reservists, transferred me off flying status with no explanation given.

Whatever the motive for this—the Marine Corps claimed it was for my "protection" as well as protection of the Corps—it provided an opening to bring in congressmen and noted lawyer F. Lee Bailey. This jarred loose, for the first time, some insight into the case against me.

In the summer of 1967, the case, primarily prepared by the navy, was bulked up by contributions from the Air Force, FBI and DINS (Directorate for Inspection Services, a watchdog group that is now defunct) and was forwarded to the Justice Department for prosecution. The role of the DINS is also a bit mysterious, and their participation outside of that identified in the Greene letter is unknown. Research on the nature of the organization turned up almost no information of value when I was putting together this book.

By the time the package was turned over to Justice, it had grown to perhaps a sizable 500 to a thousand pages of secret and top-secret documents in eleven volumes. It then sat at Justice for many months.

Finally, in early January 1969, I learned that they had decided against prosecution in February or March 1968, some ten or eleven months earlier. The Justice decision, which took place behind closed doors with no notification to me, was typical of the secrecy shrouded my case.

The Marine Corps continued to defend its position in response to reporters' questions, that I had violated some vaguely defined regulations and printed classified information after being told not to, right up to the decision point where the board's findings could either be rejected and a new board convened, or a positive judgment could be rendered.

The commandant chose the politically expedient path of approving the board's recommendation that I be retained in the Reserve and not be discharged. However, in a face-saving gesture, he followed it with a rejection of the board's many positive findings based on very flimsy premises.

The commandant, who was apparently determined not to lose a battle with a low-ranking reservist, later took steps to eliminate any promotion to a higher rank by placing significant negative information in my promotion jacket and included a caveat that any promotion must be cleared with CMC. With the help of the navy's Board for Correction of Naval Records, this maneuver was turned back.

The board sided with me and required the Marine Corps to remove the material right before the next promotion board met in February 1972. I then was selected for advancement to lieutenant colonel and at a subsequent promotion board was advanced to colonel, retiring in 1984 with twenty-seven years of active and reserve duty.

It appeared that the Navy's tenacious attitude was founded on the belief that an active reserve naval aviator on the staff of the world's premier aerospace magazine provided an inside tunnel to classified information. This suspicion was never validated and, in fact, was completely refuted during the discharge board hearing.

Since there never had been any evidence of wrongdoing on my part despite the massive effort to turn over every rock and explore every cranny, the Marine Corps, once the case became public, was forced to respond to inquiring reporters with a vague declaration that I had violated security regulations by publishing classified information that was helpful to the enemy.

The list of regulations that supposedly were violated included the voluntary reporting guidelines in Vietnam as well as naval regulations. A great deal of time was spent during the hearing to rebut these claims and the discharge board was convinced that I had done nothing wrong, either as a reporter or as a Reserve officer.

It is notable that no other organization that I dealt with, including the Defense Department, ever complained to *Aviation Week*. This was verified in a letter from Hotz at the hearing. Included was the Military Assistance Command Vietnam, which controlled the news media and published the guidelines for Vietnam reporting. In addition, there was the army and the air force neither of which came forth with complaints. The fact that sensitive information appeared in my stories reflected first-rate reporting and not illegal scrounging around in classified files.

In digging into the navy's background on handling classified information, I discovered a book titled *The Reminiscences of Adm. David Lamar McDonald, USN (Ret.)*, published in 1976 by the US Naval Institute.

McDonald was the Chief of Naval Operations (CNO), the navy's top sailor, from August 1, 1963, to August 1, 1967, when much of my case was being actively pursued. McDonald was a naval aviator who had served a lengthy period with the navy going back to the early 1930s when he served a tour onboard the carrier *Saratoga* in an exercise involving the launch of simulated air attacks on Pearl Harbor. Also on the *Saratoga,* according to McDonald, was aviation pioneer and author Grover Loening. He observed the events and wrote an article on the exercise published by the local media in Hawaii.

It was assumed that the Japanese counsel located in Hawaii had forwarded the write-up to his headquarters in Japan. McDonald then went on to point out that in analyzing the aftermath of the actual Pearl Harbor attack on December 7, 1941, that the Japanese had followed the same pattern established in the US naval exercise, almost maneuver for maneuver.

McDonald went on to say, "Of course, back then, some people tried to be careful, but we have people today in the media who seem to take great delight in publishing everything, especially if it is classified as secret, and they don't seem to care whether it might have a bad impact on our country or not." This statement was not a smoking gun that he had me in mind, but it was a good hint about his feelings and perhaps was a reference to my reporting for *Aviation Week.* The Loening incident that may have provided a path for the Japanese to plan their attack could explain the mind-set favoring tight security that prevailed in the navy.

However, in my case both the navy and marine corps had veered off on erroneous pathways in their handling of my case and only were returned to the proper course when forced to by the corrective measures imposed by the discharge and correction of records boards.

Appendix I

**The Complete Report of the
Administrative Discharge Board**

MARINE CORPS AIR STATION

EL TORO (SANTA ANA), CALIFORNIA 92709

15 August 1969

From: Administrative Discharge Board

To: Commanding General, Marine Corps Air Station, El Toro (Santa Ana), California

Subj: Administrative Discharge Board; case of Major Clemens M. PLATTNER, 062564, U.S. Marine Corps Reserve, report of

Ref: (a) Your appointing order 607:GWB:mgs over 1900 of 14 July 69

      (b) Our ltr of 7 Aug 69 requesting extension of time to report and your endorsement thereon

      (c) SECNAVINST 1900.2 dtd 24 May 55

(d) CMC ltr to Major PLATTNER of 11 Mar 69 w/enclosures (1) and (2) and attachments (1), (2), and (3)

Encl: (1) Reference (a)

(2) Reference (b)

(3) Exhibit 1 (reference(d)

(4) Exhibit 2 (ltr from PLATTNER to CG, MCAS of 22 Apr 69)

(5) Exhibit 3 (CG, MCAS ltr of 12 May 69 to PLATTNER)

(6) Exhibit 4 (MCAS ltr to O'ROURKE of 16 June 69)

(7) Exhibit 5 (MCAS ltr to O'ROURKE of 31 Jul 69)

(8) Exhibit 6 (O'ROURKE ltr to MCAS of 29 Jul 69)

(9) Exhibit 7 (MCAS ltr to O'ROURKE of 30 Jul 69)

(10) Exhibit 8 (MCAS ltr to O'ROURKE of 6 Aug 69)

(11) Exhibit 9 (1st amend on CG, MCAS ltr of 25 Apr 69)

(12) Exhibit 10 (CG, MCAS ltr to CG, 3d MAW of 25 Apr 69)

(13) Exhibit 11 (Memo to O'ROURKE from MCAS of 7 Aug 69)

(14) Exhibit A (Respondent's contentions of CMC against him)

(15) Exhibit B (excerpts of ltrs from CMC to various congressmen)

(16) Exhibit C (Respondent's ltr of 5 Aug 69 demand for discovery and MCAS ltr of 6 Aug 69 in reply)

(17) Exhibit D (PLATTNER'S ltr to CMC requesting opportunity

to reply to comment on charges with 1st and 3rd endorsements thereon)

(18) Exhibit E (PLATTNER ltr to CMC of 16 Feb 67 requesting mast)

(19) Exhibit F (CMC ltr to PLATTNER of 31 Mar 67 denying mast)

(20) Exhibit G (O'ROURKE ltr of 6 Aug 69 requesting witness)

(21) Exhibit H (ltr of editor *AW&ST* to PLATTNER OF 9 May 69 advising that no formal or informal complaint had been received concerning his articles)

(22) Exhibit I (MACV handout of "5 o'clock follies" of 8 Nov 65)

(23) Exhibit J (Article by Wilson in 10 Jan 66 AW&ST titled "US Pilots may Face New SAM radar")

(24) Exhibit K (Article from *Time* magazine of 17 Dec 65, p. 29 titled "Sam the Sham")

(25) Exhibit L (Article by Getler in *Missiles & Rockets* of 18 Oct 65 titled "DOD Re-evaluates Tactical Missiles")

(26) Exhibit M (Article from *Time* magazine of 12 Nov 65 titled "Find 'Em and Fight 'Em")

(27) Exhibit N (Article by Miller in *AW&ST* of 6 Dec 65entitled "Studies Seek Improved ASM Guidance")

(28) Exhibit O (Copy of portion of PLATTNER'S TWIX on 24 Jan 66 article in *AW&ST* with marked portion attributed to other staff members)

(29) Exhibit P (*Fighter Weapons* Newsletter, December Issue 1964 NR4 prepared by the O&T Division of the USAF Weapons School and distributed by Director of Publications 12AF re F-100 Pitch-Up Tactics)

(30) Exhibit Q (Article by Brown in 27 Dec 65 *AW&ST* entitled "A-6A Fills Interdiction Mission in Vietnam")

(31) Exhibit R (*Jane's All the World's Aircraft* corrected to July 1, 1965, on Republic AP-63-31 Thunderchief (USAF: F-105))

(32) Exhibit S (Picture of KC-135 refueling F-105 from 27 Sep 65 *AW&ST* article (p. 35) and a note from 23 Aug 65 article in *AW&ST* re same)

(33) Exhibit T (Box article from 10 Jan 66 issue *AW&ST* re F-105 missions and losses)

(34) Exhibit U (Box article in *AW&ST* issue of 23 Jan 67, p. 11, re Viet aircraft losses including SAM)

(35) Exhibit V (CMC ltr to PLATTNER of 13 Apr 67 re correspondence)

(36) Exhibit W (CMC ltr to Senator Kuchel of 21 Aug 67)

(37) Exhibit X (CMC ltr to Senator Mondale of 12 Sep 67)

(38) Exhibit Y (PLATTNER ltr to CMC of 18 June 68 re request for information)

(39) Exhibit Z (CMC ltr AIA-3-jlv of 21 May 69 to Representative Langen)

(40) Summarized Transcript of Administrative Discharge Board proceedings 4–8 Aug 1969

1. In accordance with references (a) and (b), subject Administration Discharge Board convened at 0900 on 4 August 1969 at Marine Corps Air Station, El Toro (Santa Ana), California.

2. Present were the members, Colonel Frank L. EDDENS, Jr., Colonel Collin RUSHFELDT, Colonel William A. DOUGHERTY; the recorder, Captain C. W. BEAUDRY; Major Clemens M. PLATTNER, respondent; Mr. Francis J. O'ROURKE, his civilian counsel, and Captain J. M. CAMPBELL, appointed military counsel for the respondent; Mrs. Edna L. EDWARDS, a reporter for the board, and Mr. Tom MULLEN and Mr. Bill WORLEY, certified court reporters for the respondent.

3. The board was conducted in accordance with reference (c). The summary of the information contained in reference (d) and Exhibits 2–11 were submitted to the board by the recorder (enclosures (1)-(13).

4. The respondent submitted Exhibits A–Z (enclosures (14)–(39)) to the board and presented Bruce PETERSON, Research Engineer and Test Pilot for NASA, Major George CANNON, USMCR, Irving STONE, former bureau chief for *Aviation Week & Space Technology*, and Colonel Lewis BASS, USMCR, as witnesses. All witnesses were sworn. The respondent testified under oath.

5. The respondent's service and background are as follows:

> Major Clemens M. PLATTNER was born May 29, 1930, in Walker, Minnesota. He is thirty-nine years old, the oldest of three children. His father and mother operate three weekly newspapers in Northern Minnesota.
> Major PLATTNER received a Bachelor of Arts degree from Carleton College, Northfield, Minnesota, in 1952. His major was mathematics. He was a football quarterback and ski team captain.

In August 1952, he entered the Naval Aviation Cadet Program, earned his wings and was commissioned a second lieutenant in December 1953. His flying proficiency grades were outstanding.

He served on active duty until August 1956, when he was transferred to a Class II pilot's billet at NAS, Minneapolis, Minnesota. During his active duty, he was assigned to VMC-2, MCAS, Cherry Point, flying the AD-4W and AD-4N, made a deployment to Guantanamo Bay, Cuba, and served fourteen months with MAG-33 in Korea as an assistant engineering officer. While on active duty, his fitness reports were all excellent to outstanding. Maj. Gen. Clayton C. JEROME at MCAS, El Toro, gave him a letter of commendation on his return from Korea.

At Minneapolis, he flew the Douglas A-1, Grumman F9F-5 and the Fairchild C-119.

When he was attached to the Minneapolis Reserve Squadron, he worked in the family newspaper in Walker, Minnesota, as a journeyman newspaper and printer-composer. He also attended a graduate course in journalism at the University of Minnesota.

In August of 1962, he went to work for *Aviation Week & Space Technology* magazine, a part of McGraw-Hill Publications. He trained on the job for three months in New York City and was then assigned to the Los Angeles Bureau, where he currently works.

In November of 1962, he joined Squadron VMA-241, NAS, Los Alamitos, and qualified in the Douglas A-4 Skyhawk.

He remained in the squadron until 31 January 1967, when he was transferred by order of the commandant to a nonpay billet in Class III. He was subsequently promoted to the rank of major, despite being under investigation by the Naval Intelligence Service.

During the time he was attached to VMA-241, he was given collateral duty as Squadron Historical Officer, a little-sought-after task. His report was submitted before the deadline—an act noteworthy in itself—and regarded by the permanent Marine Air Detachment officers as the best they had ever seen. Besides being on time, it was comprehensive, thorough, succinct and written with great skill.

As a weekend warrior, he was a "dedicated worker, not a barfly type." He always put forth his best effort and then did just a little more to make a better squadron and consequently a finer Marine Corps.

Major Bruce PETERSON, USMCR, a class II reservist at NAS, Los Alamitos, and a research engineer with NASA in civilian life, testified he had known Major PLATTNER since 1963; that Major PLATTNER's reputation for truth and veracity was excellent, and that he had a reputation for going to great lengths to assure accuracy in his reporting.

Major PETERSON testified that the Douglas A-4 Skyhawk was not classified in 1965 and that the Israeli and Argentine air forces were flying it. He stated it was common knowledge in 1965 that the Grumman A6A Intruder was used on Pathfinder missions and electronic countermeasure missions. He further stated that all the specifications of the Republic F-105 Thunderchief were listed in *Jane's All the Worlds Aircraft*.

Major PETERSON finally stated Major PLATTNER has an exceptionally high reputation with NASA as a military and aviation reporter.

Major George CANNON, USMCR (Ret.), a first officer for Air California, testified that he was operations officer of MARTD, NAS, Los Alamitos during the time Major PLATTNER was in VMA-241 from 1965–1967. He knew Major PLATTNER before the latter went to Vietnam. He knew Major PLATTNER's reputation for truth and veracity to be excellent. He had never heard it questioned, either in the Marine Corps or in the civilian aviation community. He was an excellent pilot.

Major CANNON had participated in the demonstration of the pop-up maneuvers at Twenty-Nine Palms in 1963 that was given for the press. Major PLATTNER covered the demonstration in a civilian capacity for *Aviation Week & Space Technology* magazine.

Naval Intelligence Service interrogated Major CANNON regarding the four articles excerpted in the summary. He stated he had read the articles textually and, in his opinion, saw nothing classified in them. When pressed closely, he firmly stated that he saw absolutely nothing classified in the total concept of the articles. He saw nothing in the articles that would aid the enemy.

It should be noted that during the time the articles were printed in early 1966, Major CANNON was attached to Marine Air Weapons Training Unit, Air FMF Pac, a highly classified, supersensitive operation dealing with the most sophisticated of weapons, both conventional and nuclear. He held a top-secret-cryptographic security clearance.

In Major CANNON's opinion, Major PLATTNER was completely trustworthy and outstandingly loyal. He believed it was Major PLATTNER's deep sense of loyalty to his country and the US Marine Corps that caused him to go to Vietnam to write the articles. The articles contained predictions, many of which came true, and comments on how the war was conducted. Major CANNON said that the Department of Defense would take umbrage with these predictions and comments, but if tactics were not changed, the war would drag on forever. He commended Major PLATTNER for his courage in writing the articles.

Col. Louis BASS, USMCR, CO, 29th Staff Group, 4th MAW, NAS, Los Alamitos, an insurance company president in civilian life, testified he had known Major PLATTNER since the latter was a second lieutenant in VMC-2 in 1953. He had known many other people who have known Major PLATTNER, both marines and civilians. Their remarks about him have always been highly complementary. He is absolutely trustworthy and unswervingly loyal to his country, the Marine Corps and to his associates.

Colonel Bass had read the instant articles. He too saw nothing of a classified nature in them and generally corroborated Major CANNON's testimony as to both the total sense of the articles and excellence of Major PLATTNER's abilities and character.

Colonel Bass, a much-decorated combat pilot in World War II and Korea, stated that Major PLATTNER had outstanding fitness reports. As a commanding officer, he would particularly desire to have Major PLATTNER in his squadron in combat.

Mr. Irving STONE, for twenty-three years Los Angeles Bureau chief of *Aviation Week & Space Technology* magazine until he retired in 1967, stated he was Major PLATTNER's supervisor when the articles were written. He said that Major PLATTNER was a most reliable, trustworthy, honorable person who enjoyed an excellent reputation as a loyal citizen. He had excellent judgment and discretion. He knew of no one in his entire career as a journalist and editor who was more competent or more industrious in his profession than Major PLATTNER.

By any standard, Major PLATTNER's career, civilian and military, has been outstanding.

His Washington Bureau informed Major PLATTNER by teletype that the aide to the then commandant, Wallace M. Greene, Jr., was inquiring about reprints of an article he had done on marine aviation. The commandant thought the article was excellent and wished copies for all his general officers.

6. The nature of the acts, omissions or traits charged against the respondent are contained in enclosure (3).

7. The position taken by the respondent with respect to the allegations, reports or other circumstances in question and acts, omissions or traits charged therein is as follows:

a. Major PLATTNER admitted articles referred to in paragraph 2 of enclosure (3) were articles he had written, except portions on page 22 of the 24 January 1966 article (see Exhibit O, enclosure (28). This portion was added to his 24 January 1966 article by other staff members of the Washington Bureau of *AW&ST* and is as follows from the summary (enclosure (3)):

"The October mission was carried out by four A-4 jet attack aircraft preceded by a Grumman A-6A which served as the Pathfinder . . . The A-6A locked onto the site approximately three minutes after the aircraft had penetrated the general vicinity . . ."

b. Major PLATTNER testified that it was the policy of *AW&ST*:

(1) Not to attend classified sessions;

(2) Have no access to known classified information;

(3) Have nothing to do with classified information;

(4) Not to submit their notes to anyone for clearance.

c. He testified that he obtained a leave of absence from his organized Marine Corps Reserve Unit and went to Vietnam as a civilian correspondent; that he did not even carry his marine ID card with him as it was his intention to fly along on missions, and he didn't want to have any military identification on his person in the event that the Viet Cong captured him.

d. That upon arriving in Vietnam, he read the policy letters (attachments 1, 2 and 3 to the summary (enclosure (3)). He stated that he discussed them with Lieutenant Colonel BIANDI, assistant security officer for MACV, and that attachment 2 was a policy letter concerning North Vietnam only and had little application to him except as to timeliness.

e. That he made no attempt to collect classified material.

f. That in regards to paragraph 9 of the summary, he did discuss with Lt. Cdr. Raymond F. JOHNSON on board the *Kitty Hawk* after being introduced to him by the ship's informational services officer, Ensign Jon McBride; that he had a discussion with JOHNSON regarding percentages; that he had been informed by ISO for MACV that he could talk about percentages if he did not identify it with the number of aircraft; that VA-85 was the second A-6 squadron to deploy off Vietnam; that MACV was opposed to telling the total number of aircraft in a squadron; that JOHNSON gave him the numbers of aircraft availability for the last fall and the present time; that JOHNSON was "queasy" about the interview and PLATTNER informed him he would talk it over with the commanding officer and the executive officer; that he did talk with the CO and XO and said, "Here are my notes," and was informed, "Yeah, go ahead, fine." He stated that he might have indicated to JOHNSON that he was a pilot and a Marine Corps Reserve, but usually, he gave no indication that he was either a pilot or marine reservist when he talked with people.

g. That none of the information in his articles was reported from classified information and that he did not have access to classified information for the articles as a Marine Reserve or otherwise.

h. That it is his policy and that of his magazine (see also California Evidence Code, Section 1070) that a reporter will not discuss nor reveal the source of his articles.

i. That he adhered to the restrictions set forth by the American embassy.

j. He rebuts paragraph 6(a) of the summary as follows:

On the basis his stories gave the enemy no information he didn't already have, and the speculations as indicated in the predictions didn't come true, but the opposite happened.

k. He rebuts paragraph 6(b) of the summary as follows:

He gave no information regarding tactics and use of the Shrike missile. In view of the previous articles published on Shrike, it was reasonable for the enemy to expect it was in use, and he certainly would know if his radars were destroyed. His statement was the Shrike was relatively ineffective. The vague knowledge used in his article was a very general statement. He gave no percentage of number of missiles fired, that the fact this weapon was sensitive to compromise had been discussed in previously published articles relative to its limitations; that the conclusion in this subparagraph was speculative in its theory and also proved to be wrong as published in the articles which appeared in *AW&ST* of February 6, 1967, to the effect that Shrike had improved and SAM sites closed down when our aircraft pointed their noses at the SAM sites.

l.   He rebuts paragraph 6(c) of the summary as follows:

The rules for South Vietnam were that the reporter could report on what he saw and heard but could not do so for North Vietnam; that he flew on at least seven missions in South Vietnam; that many other reporters flew on similar missions, and they were reported in great detail; that the war in South Vietnam was fought in a permissive environment with the largest enemy antiaircraft weapon being 20 mm; that the information he wrote on the pop-up maneuver was from unclassified sources and a matter of common knowledge. The way he described the maneuver gave the enemy no specifics; concerning the curvilinear tracking, he considered that it was an abandoned technique and had been freely discussed with him. Once again, he provided no specifics. That the approach from 7,000 to 10,000 with minimum pullout at 3,000 was obtained from his personal observation on a mission over South Vietnam; that concerning the escort for marine helicopters, this was a matter of common knowledge of long standing; that rolling in high is a technique rather than a tactic, and he chose the words "rolling in high" rather than specific altitudes; that his articles were based on common knowledge, articles previously published and information freely provided him by combat pilots; that he was treated the same as every other reporter in Vietnam.

8.   Our opinions of paragraph 7 of the summary, after considering all the evidence, is as follows:

Re: 7(a)—SPECIFIC TACTICS OF US ATTACK AIRCRAFT

a. Use of a maximum altitude of 3,000 feet inside the SAM envelope to prevent effective use of the missiles against attacking aircraft would appear to be common sense to any qualified observer. By the same token, the use of the fastest jet aircraft available for these missions would be essential to reduce the effectiveness of antiaircraft fire enroute to the target. These would appear to be straightforward assumptions by PLATTNER, and certainly, these tactics would be obvious to the enemy being attacked without substantiation in print. In addition, testimony indicates that this tactic was common knowledge and was discussed freely on an unclassified basis while PLATTNER was in Vietnam.

b. The "pop-up" tactic against SAM sites, according to the testimony of Major CANNON, indicated demonstration of this tactic to the press as early as 1963 in Twenty-Nine Palms. It was also practiced by Los Alamitos units at least as early as the summer of 1965. The use of low-level approaches was also discussed in print in October 1965 (see Exhibit L). Also in the *New York Times* article 8 December 1965 and *Time* magazine 16 December 1965, and Exhibit P.

c. The "minimum pullout altitude of 2,500–3,000 feet" referred to in the 7 February 1966 issue of *AW&ST* is an excerpt taken from a particular mission report flown in South Vietnam by PLATTNER. He reported on what happened only on that particular mission and did not allude to US tactics in general. No mention could be found of "courses, speeds and angle of attack."

d. The abandonment of curvilinear tracking in dive-bombing tactics is common knowledge due to the reasons cited in the article and would be obvious to the enemy under attack in any event. The installation of MERS and TERS received prior reporting in *AW&ST* 27 December 1965, p. 18.

e. The use of attack aircraft for helicopter escort is not a new concept. Members of this board have flown missions similar to that described as early as 1956. This tactic is also readily apparent to enemy observers in South Vietnam, where it was used.

Re: 7(b)—COMBAT PERFORMANCE CHARACTERISTICS OF THE SHRIKE MISSILE (p. 7 of 24 January 1966 article)

a. The development contract for the Shrike missile was issued by the navy in October of 1961 to Texas Instruments.

b. The first public disclosure of Shrike occurred at China Lake, California, in 1963. This was a fire-power demonstration for President Kennedy. A reporter from the Los Angeles Bureau of *AW&ST* attended the demonstration and witnessed a Shrike launching. It was announced that the Naval Ordinance Test Station had developed Shrike to counter radar installations.

c. The limitations of Shrike were published by *AW&ST* 6 December 1965 (Exhibit N), "Studies Seek improved ASM Guidance." This article by Mr. Barry Miller discusses the use of Shrike and the problems encountered. It also sets forth plans for the development of an improved missile with which to overcome these problems.

d. An article authored by Mr. Michael Getler in the 18 October 1965 issue of *MISSILES AND ROCKETS* (Exhibit

L), "DOD reevaluates Tactical Missiles," freely discusses Shrike problems and possible enemy countermeasures. It also sets forth the improvements necessary to increase the effectiveness of anti-radiation missiles.

e. PLATTNER's testimony states that he gave no information on tactics and use of the Shrike and that it was reasonable to expect that it was in use due to the published information in Exhibit N. Only vague information was contained in his articles, with no indication of the number of missiles fired or percentages.

f. The contention that improved knowledge by the enemy would make SAMs more effective is not borne out. Rather the opposite appears to be the case with a reduction in SAM effectiveness. The Shrike appears to be a much more effective weapon as well, as indicated in *AW&ST*, 6 February 1967 article by Mr. Cecil Brownlow "USAF Boost North Viet ECM Jamming."

Re: 7(c)—PERFORMANCE CHARACTERISTICS AND US COUNTERMEASURES TO SOVIET SURFACE-TO-AIR MISSILES

a. The performance characteristics and the US countermeasures to Soviet surface-to-air missiles were completely discussed in an article of 17 December 1965 in *Time* magazine. The article was "SAM the Sham." It stated that 150 missiles had downed only nine US planes. It explained evasive action taken by US jets and gave the range of SAM as twenty-eight miles (Exhibit K).

b. An article in *MISSILES AND ROCKETS* November 15, 1965, titled "DOD Re-evaluates Tactical Missiles," stated that the threat of SAMs forced US aircraft to lower altitudes, where they ran into stiff and effective conventional antiaircraft gunfire (Exhibit L).

c. *Time* magazine, November 12, 1965, in an article, "Find 'Em and Fight 'Em," described an attack on a SAM site by air force F-105s led by an electronically sensitive A-4E "Pathfinder" specially designed to snoop out missile sites (Exhibit M). A similar article appeared in the *New York Times,* December 12, 1965.

d. An article in the *New York Times* on December 21, 1965, told how the air force had switched to the F-100 as a Pathfinder because of its greater range.

e. Major PLATTNER did not write the reference to the Grumman A-6A as a Pathfinder in his article of 24 January 1966. It was added by the editor, but a prior article on the same subject had appeared in *AW&ST* on 27 December 1965 (Exhibit Q).

f. The pop-up technique has been covered in paragraph 8 above re: Paragraph 7(a) of the summary and the article in *Fighter Weapons* newsletter, December 1964 (Exhibit P).

Re: 7(d)—IDENTIFICATION OF THE NORTH AMERICAN F-100 AS PATHFINDER AIRCRAFT

a. An article in the *New York Times* dated 21 December 1965 identifies the F-100 as a Pathfinder aircraft when it was shot down while acting as a Pathfinder aircraft for a flight of F-105s. The use of Pathfinder aircraft dates back at least to the Korean Conflict.

Re: 7(e)—BOMB BAY CONFIGURATION OF THE F-105

a. PLATTNER contends that no information concerning the bomb bay configuration was published that did not appear in *Jane's All the World's Aircraft* (corrected to 1 July 1965). This article states that the F-105 was developed to meet USAF requirements for a supersonic single-seat fighter bomber able to deliver nuclear weapons and heavier loads of conventional bombs and rockets at very high speeds and over long ranges.

b. The article also refers to an alternate fuel tank with a capacity of 300 US gallons (approximately 2,500 lbs) located in the bomb bay. In addition, it refers to several typical armament loads.

Re: 7(f)—LOSS RATES OF F-105 and A-4

a. The loss rate of the F-105 had been previously declared in an article, not written by Major PLATTNER, in *AW&ST,* January 10, 1966 (Exhibit T).

b. The reference to the loss ratio of the A-4 was provided by the Washington Office of *AW&ST* in an article on December 27, 1965, p 13.

Re: 7(g)—STATEMENTS AS TO THE OPERATIONAL READINESS RATE (page 83 of 21 February 1966 article)

a. Excerpts from the 21 February 1966 article in the summary furnished this board (Exhibit I) contained nothing in reference to operational readiness rates.

Re: 7(h)—STATEMENT THAT ELECTRONIC INTELLIGENCE MISSIONS BEING FLOWN BY DOUGLAS AIRCRAFT (page 83 of 21 February 1966 article)

  a. Excerpts from the 21 February 1966 article in the summary furnished this board (Exhibit 1) contains nothing in reference to electronic intelligence missions flown by Douglas aircraft.

  b. It is noted that the article from *Time* magazine of 12 November 1965 mentions a flight of F-105s being led by an electronically sensitive A-4E "Pathfinder" specially designed to snoop out missile sites (Exhibit M).

9. **Our conclusions, based upon all the evidence available to the board, are as follows:**

  a. The allegation that the information divulged in the articles was "significantly beneficial to the enemy" was apparently provided Headquarters, Marine Corps, by DOD (DINS), and the Naval Investigative Service Headquarters. The board concludes that no information of a classified nature was contained in the summary excerpts (Exhibit 1) since prior published articles would indicate the enemy had prior access to the subject alleged disclosures.

  b. Major PLATTNER was physically in Vietnam only by virtue of his status as an accredited correspondent. The nature of this status exposed him to information not generally available to those reporters who were not in Vietnam. Apparently, DOD presumed that certain information picked up in this capacity was protected by the policy letters of the American embassy. The policy letter (attachments 2 and 3 to the summary (Exhibit 1)) merely requested correspondents to abide by the stated policy voluntarily in the interest of military security. It is noted that attachment 2 (Release of Air Strike Information) referred to above applies to the release of information on air strikes in North Vietnam only, whereas attachment 3 (Release of Combat Information) applies to the release of information on South Vietnam. We find no violation by Major PLATTNER from the policies stated in these two attachments.

c. No regulation compels a member of the press to submit his material for security review.

d. The rule of "security at the source" puts the onus on those who reveal the information rather than the recipient. Major PLATTNER was willingly and specifically issued all the information in question. He was at the source of the information itself and was free to travel around and to view events as they occurred. He was allowed the freedom to view events and to inquire about them. His only restrictions on his articles were governed by the policy issued by the American embassy, which is referred to in paragraph 9(b) above. There is no evidence that he used Marine Corps Reserve status to gain any information.

10. **In view of the entire record compiled by this board, it is recommended that Major PLATTNER be retained in the Marine Corps Reserve. His loyalty to our country and the Marine Corps has been proved conclusively. His retention in the Marine Corps Reserve will be a valuable asset to the service.**

Respectfully submitted,

_____

Frank L. Eddens, Colonel, USMCR

_____

Collin Rushfeldt, Colonel, USMCR

_____

William A. Dougherty, Colonel, USMCR

Appendix 2

ENCLOSURE (2) OF CMC LETTER DATED 11 MAR 1969
TO MAJOR CLEMENS PLATTNER, TITLED
"SUMMARY OF INFORMATION IN THE CASE OF
MAJ. CLEMENS MAESER PLATTNER, USMCR, 062564"

1. The Assistant Secretary of Defense for Public Affairs requested an investigation of PLATTNER for authoring a number of articles that appeared in the *Aviation Week & Space Technology* (*AW&ST*) and divulged detailed tactical and logistical information. In connection therewith, the Naval Investigative Service (Department of the Navy) and office of Special Investigations (Department of Air Force) conducted inquiries under the overall coordination of the Directorate for Inspection Services, Office of Assistant Secretary for Defense for Administration.

2. Preliminary inquiry identified the articles in question as:

   - "SAMs Spur Changes in Combat Tactics, New Equipment" in 24 Jan 1966 issue of *AW&ST*

   - "Combat Dictates Shift in Navy Air Tactics" in 7 Feb 1966 issue of *AW&ST*

   - "Marine Control of Air Tested in Combat" in 14 Feb 1966 issue of *AW&ST*

- "North Viet Sortie Rate Pressed as Political Purpose Fails" in 21 Feb 1966 issue of *AW&ST*

3. All of the foregoing articles, which bear PLATTNER's byline, appeared to be at least partially based on information obtained by PLATTNER during his visit to the Republic of Vietnam (RVN) during October–December 1965. PLATTNER entered RVN on 21 October 1965 and was accredited as a correspondent on 22 October 1965 at COMUSMACV Public Affairs Office, Saigon. He remained in RVN until approximately 20 December 1965.

4. PLATTNER acknowledged, by signature, his receipt of COMUSMACV policy letters containing guidelines as to categories of information that should not be published for reasons of military security. Attachment (1) is a "Correspondents Data Sheet" submitted by PLATTNER on 22 October 1965. Attachments (2) and (3) are copies of policy letters titled "Release of Air Strike Information" and "Release of Combat Information," which PLATTNER acknowledged receiving. It is noted that restrictions to be observed for security reasons included: specific tactical details such as altitudes, courses, speeds, angle of attack and aircraft losses.

5. The following excerpts, relating to aircraft tactics, losses and combat maneuvers in apparent violation of the COMUSMACV policy letters, were contained in PLATTNER's articles of 24 January, 7 February, 14 February and 21 February 1966 issues of *Aviation Week & Space Technology* magazine:

24 January 1966 Issue

"These Russian SA-2 missiles, although directly responsible for downing only ten US aircraft, registering a kill rate of 5 percent for all missiles fired, have, nevertheless, forced tactical aircraft to fly at lower altitudes where the probability of being hit by conventional antiaircraft fire is increased."

"Pathfinder aircraft equipped with radar-homing devices began to be used last fall in a 'hunter-killer' role. The Pathfinder pinpointed an active SAM site by flying over it, and the strike aircraft following it deliver bombs and rockets on the site."

"First aircraft to be used successfully as a Pathfinder was the Navy/Douglas A-4. The A-4s were used as Pathfinders for both Republic/USAF F-105s as well as navy strike aircraft. The Air Force installed a radar-homing device on the F-105, but it turned out to be ineffective, largely because of limited range. USAF then switched to a North American F-100 as a Pathfinder."

"Conventional bombs and unguided missiles are being used to knock out the SAM sites since the Shrike missile, developed for silencing radar transmitters, has proven relatively ineffective. It is felt that most Shrikes have failed to strike the target, although there were cases where the radar stopped emitting signals. It is not known whether this was a countermeasures move, however, or whether the Shrike had blown up the radar unit."

"SA-2s are generally ineffective against aircraft flying at high speeds at altitudes under 3,000 ft. This makes the use of jet aircraft almost mandatory since slower aircraft such as the Douglas A1 are easier to hit and consequently are not used inside the Sam envelope"

"The October mission was carried out by four A-4 jet attack aircraft preceded by a Grumman A-6A which served as the Pathfinder . . . The A-6A locked onto the site approximately three minutes after the aircraft had penetrated the general vicinity . . ."

"Both services now frequently use the pop-up maneuver on missions against SAM sites and other heavily defended targets within the SAM envelope. Navy units striking these targets have all abandoned rolling in on runs from high altitude, a favored technique prior to the advent of the SAM missiles and radar-controlled antiaircraft guns."

"The pop-up technique was developed during the Cuban Missile Crisis in late 1962 but was not widely practiced subsequently. It involves a final run to the target at a low level to escape radar detection. A pull-up is made just short of the target, and at the top of the pull-up, the aircraft is rolled and pulled through to place the sight on the target and a normal dive-bombing run is completed."

"This pop-up maneuver involves precise navigation to the pull-up point, which may be directly in line with the target or more often slightly offset, requiring a modified barrel roll or wingover to establish the aircraft in its run."

"Acquiring the target is one of the most difficult tasks to master since the pilot sees the target for the first time during the pull-up and has only a short time to become oriented and place his aircraft into an aiming trajectory. This compares with the normal mission in South Vietnam where aircraft approach the target at 7,000–10,000 ft. and have several minutes during an orbit of the target to identify it clearly."

7 February 1966 Issue

"The A-4 also has been hit the most, and more A-4s than any other navy aircraft have been lost, although there has been a loss rate per sorties of only about .002 in strikes against North Vietnamese targets."

"Minimum pullout altitude was 2,500–3,000 ft., well about the fragmentation pattern of the 250-lb bomb. Normal 30-degree dives were used."

"Complete weapons system availability rate for the A-6 rose from 10–20 percent in the fall of 1964 to about 50 percent last fall, and availability of the aircraft for VFR missions rose from 40–50 percent in the same period to 70 percent."

". . . a particularly valuable technique for locating enemy targets during low-altitude entry to avoid radar detection is to use specially equipped aircraft as Pathfinders. The two aircraft used so far in this role are: A6A, which is used because of its excellent radar system. A-6s are not fitted with special electronic countermeasures equipment."

"A4C and E aircraft fitted with radar-homing devices used to lead both navy and USAF aircraft on SAM strikes. Other navy aircraft are equipped with electronic countermeasures gear capable of detecting when a SAM is fired. This permits a warning to be sounded that SAMs are being launched and alerts pilots to watch for them. Other electronic countermeasures equipment now in use permits jamming the radar control systems of antiaircraft guns."

"Navy has had to revise some tactics which didn't work out well . . ., the following technique is no longer generally practiced: curvilinear or pipper-to-target tracking in dive-bombing runs. This tracking technique involves keeping the pipper of the gun sight continually pointed at the target rather than maintaining a constant dive angle and walking it up to the target as is normally done. With pipper-to-target tracking, an arcing trajectory is flown as the dive angle increases due to the buildup in airspeed. Several A-6s were lost to this technique as the bombs after release collided with the aircraft, which had to maintain a slight negative g to stay in the dive. Although the accidents happened prior to the installation of MERs and TERs, which forcefully eject the bombs away from the aircraft, the technique has been abandoned. The advent of radar-controlled antiaircraft guns of 87 and 100 mm forced abandonment of the technique of rolling in on targets from high altitudes."

14 February 1966 Issue

"The missions flown by marine jets in support of marine operations break down as follows: *Ground-controlled radar bombing missions* known as TPQ-10 missions. These are straight and level-bombing missions flown by F-4B or A-4C and E aircraft under the direction of portable ground radar units assigned to Marine Air Support Squadrons. About one-third of marine A-4 and F-4 missions are TPQ-10 radar-controlled bombing missions. They are flown predominantly at night against suspected Viet Cong targets with a reported circular error probability (CEP) less than 150 meters. Results of these TPQ sorties are usually unknown to the pilots who fly them since damage assessment is seldom made, but the harassment effect against the Viet Cong is considered important. Pilots feel TPQ missions are the most boring they fly in the air-to-ground role since their bombs are dropped from 10,000–20,000 ft. in straight and level flight—similar in many respects to the way the Boeing B-52s drop their bombs."

"*Helicopter escort.* About one-third of the marine A-4 missions are helicopter escorts, with a somewhat smaller percentage of F-4 missions flown in this way due to the air defense commitment shared with the Air Force at Danang. The Marine Corps with direct control over its aircraft as well as helicopters is the only service which routinely uses jets to escort helicopters to landing zones, although USAF has evaluated the tactic."

"Normally, three marine jets accompany helicopters enroute flying a translating circular profile or a 'snake dance' pattern overhead so that one aircraft is always in a position to make a run on any enemy antiaircraft gun which may fire on the helicopters. A typical marine helicopter landing assault consists of A-4 escort aircraft, armed UH-1Es and an Air Force forward air controller flying a Cessna O-1 to direct the jets. Sometimes, the pilots of the UH-1Es act as airborne forward air controllers, but the former concept of the lead helicopter pilot acting as a forward air controller calling targets for the jets has been abandoned. Using jets to accompany helicopters has had a deterrent effect on the Viet Cong who initially fired frequently at the helicopters but now rarely do so except in the landing zone."

"*Reconnaissance missions* over North Vietnam by Ling-Temco-Vought RF-8As and Douglas EF-10Bs (formerly F-3D Skynights) of the VMCJ squadron, requiring escort by F-4s. These are the only missions flown over North Vietnam by marine aircraft."

21 February 1966 Issue

"F-105 operation highlights include the following: Bomb bay designed to house a nuclear store has been filled with a 2,500-lb capacity fuel tank for extra range. All missions are flown with external fuel in one of two configurations—either two 450-gal drop tanks on inboard pylons or one 650-gal drop tank on the centerline. The normal load with the two drop tanks is six 750-lb M117 bombs or five 1,000-lb MK83 bombs. With the single centerline tank, two 2,000- or 3,000-lb bombs can be carried. The maximum gross takeoff weight of the F-105 is 52,800 lb.   Refueling is conducted on most missions. Short radius strikes last just over two hrs, and long radius missions run about three and a half hrs. Two midair refueling are conducted on long radius missions against targets in the northeastern part of North Vietnam. Water injection is used on almost every takeoff, which normally is with the full fuel load. Water injection boosts rated takeoff thrust of the Pratt and Whitney J75-P-19W to 26,500 lb. with an afterburner. The J75, a heavy, rugged engine, has been able to absorb considerable damage from foreign objects and keep running at least long enough to make it to an emergency landing site"

"The supersonic speed capability of the F-105 has proved to be of little use in the war. Normally, F-4Cs provide high cover fighter escorts for the F-105s. Philco Sidewinder missiles are almost never carried, and pilots rarely can fly supersonically. The F-105, like all other tactical jet aircraft, flies subsonically in the conventional delivery role."

"Between 75 percent and 80 percent of air force strike missions are flown by the F-105, and loss rates have been correspondingly high. Some squadrons have lost as many as 30 percent of their aircraft over six months, and more than sixty F-105s have been lost over the past year (*AW&ST*, Jan. 10, p. 33). The F-105 loss rate for out-of-country missions has averaged .005."

"Gun pods are sometimes carried on F-4C escort missions, but for long-range flights or when loiter time is needed, the pod is left off because of its high drag."

"Speed and surprise are the two principal advantages which US strike aircraft have against the antiaircraft defense in North Vietnam. The 'pop-up maneuver' (*AW&ST*, Jan 24, p. 31) is most often employed against heavily defended targets. However, both air force and navy still prefer to roll in high against poorly defended targets when possible."

"6. On 21 March 1966, the Air Warfare Division of the Office of the Chief of Naval Operations (OP-05) summarized the significance of the disclosures as follows:

"a. *Surface-to-Air Missiles*—The enemy can now be expected to have *confirmed data* on operational kill rates, inadequacies of SA-2 missiles, US means of establishing missile alerts, US efforts to hunt and kill SAM equipment, potential SAM and AAA tactical changes, which will raise the combined kill rate, and US methods of electronic countermeasure used. This accumulation of performance could enable him to alter his SA-2 firing tactics and make changes in SA-2 systems, increasing the kill potential of the weapon and force significantly higher loss rates upon US attack aircraft.

"b. *SHRIKE Anti-Radiation Missiles*—The enemy can now be expected to have improved knowledge of US tactics and US effectiveness in using this new weapon. This weapon is particularly sensitive to compromise. And changes, either tactical or technical, in the enemy's use of his radars, could decrease the weapon's effectiveness.

The ultimate effects may be to render an important US weapon ineffective, to permit the enemy a lower attrition of his radars and provide a correspondingly higher effectiveness of the enemy ground radar antiaircraft warning and defense system.

"c. *Tactics of US Attack Aircraft*—The enemy can now be expected to have a broader and deeper knowledge of the tactics US attack aircraft are employing. Speeds, altitudes, roll-in points, pullout 'Gs,' release altitudes, communications procedures and similar briefing details are stated. A military pilot faced with continued flying duties in this hostile environment would not be inclined to divulge similar information because of the resultant obvious possible improvement of enemy capability."

"7. At the time the above-mentioned data was published under PLATTNER'S byline, the following items of information were being protected as classified information within the military services but have since been declassified:

"(a) Specific tactics of US attack aircraft (various pages)

"(b) Combat performance characteristics of SHRIKE anti-radiation missile (page 27 of 24 Jan 1966 article)

"(c) Performance characteristics and US countermeasures to Soviet surface-to-air missiles (various pages of 24 Jan 1966 article)

"(d) Identification of North American F-100 as a Pathfinder (page 27 of 24 Jan 1966 article)

"(e) Bomb bay configuration of F-105 (page 83 of 21 Feb 1966 article)

"(f) Statements concerning loss rates of F-105 (page 83 of 21 Feb 1966 article) and A-4 (page 65 of 7 Feb 1966 article)

"(g) Statements as to operational readiness rate (page 83 of 21 Feb 1966 article)

"(h) Statements that electronic intelligence missions being flown by Douglas aircraft (page 83 of 21 Feb 1966 article)"

"8. Although investigation disclosed no instance in which he directly solicited classified data from military interviewees by virtue of his SECRET clearance in the Marine Corps Reserve, it was disclosed that on at least one occasion, PLATTNER led a military officer whom he was interviewing to believe that he would submit his notes or manuscripts for a security review by a higher military echelon prior to publication. Based on that assurance, sensitive information was divulged to PLATTNER. There was no record of PLATTNER submitting manuscripts of the four articles for security review by military authorities prior to publication."

"9. During questioning on 5 May 1966, Lt. Cdr. Raymond F. JOHNSON, Jr., USN, stated that PLATTNER interviewed him in Ready Room #3 aboard the USS *KITTY HAWK* for about 30–45 minutes during the fall of 1965. Lt. Cdr. JOHNSON said that he tried to hold the conversation to routine matters; however, PLATTNER wished to discuss maintenance aspects of the A-6 aircraft. During this discussion, PLATTNER identified himself to Lieutenant Commander JOHNSON as an attack pilot in the Marine Corps Reserve. Lieutenant Commander JOHNSON believed that PLATTNER had shown him a reserve identification card. When requested to furnish the availability figure for the A-6 aircraft, Lieutenant Commander JOHNSON at first refused to do so due to its CONFIDENTIAL security classification. However, PLATTNER assured him that COMUSMACV allowed him to quote percentages and that COMUSMACV would ultimately screen his notes. On the strength of this, Lt. Cdr. JOHNSON then answered the question by stating, '75 percent of the time, 50 percent for all-weather missions.' In further discussions, Lt. Cdr. JOHNSON recalled commenting to PLATTNER concerning radar reliability; however, he declined to discuss electronic countermeasures or armaments. At the conclusion of the interview, Lt. Cdr. JOHNSON recalled that he recommended to his commanding officer, Cdr. B. J. CARTWRIGHT, USN, and his executive officer, Cdr. J. E. KELLER, USN, that PLATTNER'S notes should be reviewed for security purposes before he left the *KITTY HAWK*. Lieutenant Commander Johnson recalled seeing PLATTNER show his notes to COMMANDER KELLER thereafter but did not hear what transpired. According to Lieutenant Commander JOHNSON, both COMMANDER CARTWRIGHT and COMMANDER KELLER were later killed in action."

"10. On 8 October 1966, agents of Naval Investigative Service contacted PLATTNER to arrange a private interview concerning this matter. He immediately queried the agents about whether it concerned an article he published in relation to his Vietnam trip and commented to the effect that, if so, he had "literary license" and would not divulge his sources of information. However, he agreed to meet the agents on 10 October 1966 at Naval Investigative Service Resident Agency, Pasadena, California. Subsequently, PLATTNER told the agents that on advice from his editor, he wished to postpone the interview until 17 October 1966. He indicated that he had been directed to have Mr. Irving STONE, his supervisor, present during the interview, and it must take place in the Los Angeles office of *AW&ST* rather than the Naval Investigative Service Office. Since those conditions were considered unacceptable, said Naval Investigative Service canceled the interview."

"11. PLATTNER came to the attention of the Naval Investigative Service in 1963 in connection with an investigation concerning the alleged unauthorized disclosure of classified information in an article titled 'Extensive Electronics Aid A2F Capability' (*AW&ST,* 5 Nov 1962). When interviewed on 8 February 1963 at the *AW&ST* office in Los Angeles, PLATTNER insisted that Mr. Irving STONE, his supervisor, be present. During the course of the interview, STONE interrupted on several occasions, advising PLATTNER not to name his sources for the article nor furnish a formal statement concerning the matter. During questioning, PLATTNER admitted that he wrote the article in question after visiting Grumman Aircraft Corporation, denied knowing that the article contained classified data, and refused to divulge

his specific sources of information."
ATTACHMENTS

1. MACV Office of Information Special Projects Division correspondence Data Sheet of C. M. Plattner
2. COMUSMACV Policy Letter entitled "RELEASE OF AIR STRIKE INFORMATION"
3. COMUSMACV Policy Letter entitled "RELEASE OF COMBAT INFORMATION"